If We Will...
Then He Will

A 50 State Prayer Project

II Chronicles 7:14

If My people, who are called by My name, will humble themselves and pray and seek My face and turn from their wicked ways, then I will hear from heaven, and I will forgive their sin and will heal their land.

Painted Gate Publishing

ISBN 978-1-952465-17-8

Prayer
lays hold of
God's plan *and*
becomes the link
between **His will**
and its accomplishment
on earth.

- Elisabeth Elliot

We thought it was just lunch. But God had something else in mind.

We are three women acquaintances from church who just decided to have lunch. 15 minutes into lunch, one of us said she had been asking the Lord for a couple of friends to help with an idea she believed was of the Lord. She explained a plan to organize prayer warriors from each State to pray over America. We said "Let's do it!" The flame was lit.

We felt it was too overwhelming a job for three ordinary women from South Dakota. But if it was the Lord's will, He could make it happen. And He did, in miraculous ways! He tapped each one of our unique personalities, giftings and backgrounds to bring this to fruition. After only 7 weeks, with over 70 hours of meetings and countless hours of writing and rewriting, the rough draft of this manuscript was complete.

May Almighty God use these words to stir hearts and bring revival in this nation and around the world, for His kingdom and His glory.

A Three Strand Cord (Ecclesiastes 4:12)

Table of Contents

1

THE PURPOSE

If My people, who are called by My name, will humble themselves and pray and seek My face and turn from their wicked ways, then I will hear from heaven, and I will forgive their sin and will heal their land.   II Chronicles 7:14

"If We Will...Then He Will"

If we will...then He will. What does that mean?

Many of us are feeling a growing unsettledness in our hearts. We are disturbed by the increasing immorality, division, and violence we see in our nation, and there doesn't seem to be an easy answer. We are growing fearful of the potential seismic shift in our futures.

We want our nation, our land to be healed. And that is what God promises to do, right? Yes, but it is an "If...then" proposition. "*If* we will...*then* He will." So what needs to happen *first*?

II Chronicles 7:14 tells us we *first* must humble ourselves, pray, seek His face and turn from our wicked ways. Only then will He forgive our sin and heal our land.

"If We Will…Then He Will" is a grassroots prayer project that was birthed from a desire to bring repentance and revival to the hearts of His people, those of us called by His name.

This is not motivated by politics or church affiliation. It is simply a call to His people to turn from *our* wicked ways and implore Him to heal our land. The plan prepares intercessors from all 50 states to pray for 50 days for His people and for our nation.

How? It begins on December 1 with 31 days of preparation for spiritual battle. This is followed by a time of prayer and fasting on January 1, New Year's Day. Then for 50 days - January 2 through February 20 - prayer warriors from all 50 states will be led in interceding on behalf of God's people, our nation and our world.

This is not a passive project. We have a real enemy, and we need to learn how to seriously and effectively engage in battle against him and "the spiritual forces of evil in the heavenly realms" (Ephesians 6:12). Therefore, there are 31 days of preparation for spiritual warfare, as well as a time of prayer and fasting, prior to our 50 days of intercession.

Why 50 days? The 50-day plan has specific and unique daily rotating reading assignments in Psalms for intercessors in each of the 50 states. The result is that the *entire* book of Psalms will be lifted to the Lord by intercessors all across our nation *each and every day* for 50 days. Each prayer warrior will also seek the Lord daily, asking Him for the petitions He desires we bring before Him in prayer. The details are laid out on the following pages.

There is real hope for a new beginning, but only if we do it God's way. Together, this is our journey back to Him, back to our "first love" (Revelation 2:4 KJV). Only then will we be enabled to turn from our wicked ways. And only then will He heal our land.

2

THE PROBLEM

We all, like sheep, have gone astray, each of us has turned to
our own way;... Isaiah 53:6a

How Did We Get Here??

We watched in horror and disbelief. From airplanes being used as instruments of terror on September 11, to our cities being set on fire, we thought "How did we get here??"

The answer is simple. We decided to follow our own human nature. We went astray, turning away from God and His way, His truth. We have become lovers of self...lovers of money..."lovers of pleasure rather than lovers of God" (II Timothy 3:2-4).

In the thousands of years of human history, a cycle of civilization has repeated itself over and over again. People find themselves in misery. Out of desperation, they cry out to God and experience a spiritual awakening. Delivery from misery brings liberty. Liberty, in turn, produces abundance. But sadly, abundance greatly diminishes the perception of a need for God. People begin doing what is right in their own eyes. The culture devolves into decadence as people seek more and more pleasure. And as sure as the sun rises and sets, cultures and people end up again in misery.

If we look at American history, we find a similar pattern. The great revivals of the 1700's led to great courage which bought freedom. The new nation, while not perfect, was established on Judeo-Christian values. Our founding documents reflected the founders' respect for God's moral standards. References to their dependence on Almighty God were frequent. For example, our first President, George Washington, declared "It is the duty of all nations to acknowledge the providence of Almighty God, to obey His will, to be grateful for His benefits, and humbly to implore His protection and favor." [i]

Our nation's history is filled with examples of God's protection and favor. But the resulting abundance and prosperity have predictably led to decadence. It now feels as if we are in moral freefall and headed back into misery. How sadly predictable we are.

As a nation, we have continued to turn away from God and His principles as laid out in His Word. Many believe that we have "outgrown" our need for a belief in God, declaring we don't need God - or anyone else for that matter - telling us what to do. They claim there are no moral absolutes, no real right nor wrong. They proclaim freedom to follow their own personal moral compass, that they are free to do whatever feels right in their own eyes.

Right in their own eyes? Where have we heard that concept before? It is repeated numerous times throughout Scripture as the Bible described a rebellious, "stiff-necked" people turning away from God, time and time again. And predictably, it always ends up in disaster. Those who profess to be wise become fools (Romans 1:22).

So where do we go from here? Can we stop a repeat of the cycle? Yes, but only if we experience spiritual renewal. Read on to learn more about God's way to bring that about.

3

THE PLAN

If My people, who are called by My name, will humble themselves and pray and seek My face and turn from their wicked ways, then I will hear from heaven, and I will forgive their sin and will heal their land. II Chronicles 7:14

What Can We Do About It?

II Chronicles 7:14 is a core verse that we will return to again and again. It is a concise description of God's prescription for the cure we desire, both for ourselves and our nation.

This remedy was given by God to Solomon following the dedication of Solomon's magnificent temple. Much like our nation, Israel was at its historic height of power and prosperity. So why did God choose that time to tell Solomon that His people needed to turn from their wicked ways? Because God knows human nature. He knows that, in the midst of peace and prosperity, even we, His people, can feel as though we really don't need Him, and we end up going astray, going our own way. In His love and mercy, God outlines His way for us to come back to Him.

What is God's prescription? It is pretty straightforward. It requires *our* humbling; *our* earnest prayer, seeking God with *our* whole heart, and turning from *our* wicked ways. Ouch.

We tend to think that *other* people need to stop being such sinners. Why can't *they* just turn from *their* wicked ways so we can all be blessed by God and live together in peace and harmony? Like the fairy tale, we just want to live happily ever after. We are tempted to point the finger at other people and say *their* sin is to blame. But God says it's *our* sin.

Many of us don't want to talk or even think about sin. We know the Word says "For all have sinned and fall short of the glory of God" (Romans 3:23). But we don't *really* believe that. Most of us agree we aren't perfect, but we aren't all that bad, are we? We've all made "mistakes" as we call them. But we often knew right from wrong when we chose to do wrong. Why? Because we rationalized it wasn't really all that wrong? Because we thought we could get away with it? Because everyone else did it? Or maybe just because it made us feel good?

But then the reality of our foolish and willful choices set in. The little seeds of sin, those things that felt right in our own eyes, took root in our hearts and grew until they were full blown, full grown. Then came the reaping: the broken hearts and relationships, the damaged spiritual, emotional or physical health. That wasn't part of our fairy tale. We ignored the truth that sin is pleasurable only for a season (Hebrews 11:25), but then come the consequences.

Unfortunately, there's more cold, hard truth we prefer to ignore: "Judgment must begin with the House of God" (I Peter 4:17 KJV). God's anger is particularly kindled against us, His people. Why? Because He paid the ultimate price with His life to redeem us. He opened our eyes to the truth and we experienced His grace and His goodness. And yet, in so many ways, we have chosen to turn our back on Him and go astray, go our own way. How?

Many of us as His people have lost our desire to be distinctive, to be set apart, to please Him alone. We find ourselves more focused on personal happiness and less on personal holiness. We may be choosing the comfort of lukewarm so we can straddle that fence – just enough repentance to get to heaven but just enough sin to feel good here. Many of us who call ourselves Christians are either secretly or openly in addiction to the pleasures of food, alcohol, pornography or other sexual immoralities. There now is very little difference in the moral metrics between "Christians" and the world. Is it because we have deposed God Almighty and elevated our pleasures to reign on the throne of our lives? Is that why our culture suddenly feels like a run-away train? Are *our* compromises to blame?

Some of us have spread the lie that people don't need to turn from their sin because "God will understand." Some even go so far as to teach

6

that what we used to call sin isn't even sin anymore. In an attempt to embrace the sinner, some of us have ended up endorsing the sin. And some have even joined in rebuking and mocking those who remain true to God's Word.

Jesus joins the world in calling us hypocrites; we may honor Him with our mouths, but our hearts are far from Him; we worship Him in vain and our teachings are just human rules (Matthew 15:7-9). No wonder we fear judgment is just around the corner. Because it is.

What can we do about it? God has a remedy. He is bringing us to a recognition of our need for spiritual re-awakening. That may be why you are reading this right now. You may be sensing a desperation, a fear that our world of comfort and ease is quickly falling away. This fear helps turn us from the foolishness of our ways and return to the wisdom of His ways.

"If We Will…Then He Will" shows us a way to "turn" and "return" together:

Part I consists of 31 days of preparation. Why? Because we are preparing for battle. Part I begins December 1 and ends on New Year's Eve. Each day, we will read and meditate on a different chapter of Proverbs. Why Proverbs? Because two of the greatest deficiencies in our nation are wisdom and the distinction between right and wrong. We need training and reinforcement in both areas before we head into battle. We also will be looking at several verses, including II Chronicles 7:14 and James 5:16, and topics such as the armor of God. The purpose of this preparation is to make us more fit and effective prayer warriors for our 50 days of intercession to follow.

Part II of this program is a time of prayer and fasting on New Year's Day, January 1. This day immediately precedes the 50 days of intercession. What this time of prayer and fasting will look like for you is just between you and the Lord. No one else needs to know what you are doing; but the Lord will know and promises to hear.

Part III consists of 50 days of praises, prayers and petitions, starting on January 2 and ending on February 20. We will be reading the book of Psalms as a catalyst to remind us of God's greatness, of our neediness, and of His faithfulness to answer those who cry out to Him in repentance and desperate dependence. Each daily reading in Psalms will then be followed by our praises, prayers and petitions as He leads us in intercession each day.

We can expect Him not only to hear, but also to answer our prayers. Why? Because He says so. But our nation also has amazing stories of when He has miraculously answered our prayers.

4

THE POWER

My help comes from the LORD, the Maker of heaven and earth.
Psalm 121:2

The Power of Prayer

Have there been times in history when people have cried out to God Almighty and He has answered in miraculous ways? Actually, yes.

One of the most recent and well-documented events in American and world history happened in December of 1944 during World War II's pivotal Battle of the Bulge.

General Patton wrote in his journal "Know of nothing more I can do to prepare for this attack except to read the Bible and pray." [ii] But after seeking the Lord's face, he must have been led to do more. Patton contacted the Army's Chief Chaplain, James H. O'Neill, and organized a call for all the troops to pray. The result? Six days of uncharacteristically clear weather for Europe in December, the dead of winter. Those six days of clear skies turned the tide of World War II.

Here are the fascinating details:

From September to December, fog and rain had plagued General Patton and his soldiers, limiting their use of air power. On the morning of

December 8, 1944, General Patton called the Army's Chief Chaplain, James H. O'Neill. "This is General Patton; do you have a good prayer for weather? We must do something about those rains if we are to win the war." [iii]

General Patton told the Chief Chaplain "I am a strong believer in prayer. Up to now, in the Third Army, God has been very good to us. This is because a lot of people back home are praying for us. But we have to pray for ourselves, too. We've got to get not only the chaplains but every man in the Third Army to pray. We must ask God to stop these rains. If we all pray, it will be like plugging in on a current whose source is in Heaven. It is power." [iv]

Within the hour, a prayer had been written and approved. Patton ordered 250,000 prayer cards produced, and then distributed to each soldier in the Third Army. With the presses working day and night, both the printing and distribution were accomplished by December 14, only six days after the order had been given. Each soldier had a prayer card in hand as they anxiously awaited the next battle. They did not have long to wait.

Just two days later, on December 16, 1944, German forces launched a surprise offensive, aided by the cover of "heavy rains, thick fogs and swirling ground mists that muffled sound, blotted out the sun, and reduced visibility to a few yards," wrote the Chief Chaplain. "For three days it looked to the jubilant Nazis as if their desperate gamble would succeed." [v]

But then the anguished and totally dependent prayers of the Allied soldiers facing defeat were answered with a miracle. The Chief Chaplain continues his eyewitness account:

"On December 20, to the consternation of the Germans and the delight of the American forecasters who were equally surprised at the turn-about, the rains and the fogs ceased. For the better part of a week came bright clear skies and perfect flying weather. General Patton prayed for fair weather for battle. He got it." [vi]

Prayer turned the tide. This was the prayer on that card: [vii]

PRAYER

ALMIGHTY and most merciful Father, we humbly beseech Thee, of Thy great goodness, to restrain these immoderate rains with which we have had to contend. Grant us fair weather for Battle. Graciously hearken to us as soldiers who call upon Thee that armed with Thy power, we may advance from victory to victory, and crush the oppression and wickedness of our enemies, and establish Thy justice among men and nations. Amen.

PRAYER

LMIGHTY and most merciful Father, we humbly beseech Thee, of Thy great goodness, to restrain these immoderate rains with which we have had to contend. Grant us fair weather for Battle. Graciously hearken to us as soldiers who call upon Thee that armed with Thy power, we may advance from victory to victory, and crush the oppression and wickedness of our enemies, and establish Thy justice among men and nations. Amen.

What made this prayer so miraculously powerful? It certainly wasn't the size of the card; it was only the size of a business card. It certainly wasn't the quantity of words; it could be read aloud in 30 seconds or less. It was the condition of the heart of the "pray-er" and the powerful God they were praying to. This prayer would have been prayed whole-heartedly, fervently. Imagine if we were in the trenches. It was a time of desperation, of total dependence. God was their *only* hope, their *only* salvation. And Almighty God delivered in a remarkable way.

The Nazis' attack on December 16 was a surprise to the Allied Forces. But it was not a surprise to Almighty God. God had already pre-arranged for the Third Army soldiers to have the prayer cards in hand by December 14th, two days *prior* to the surprise attack.

The Nazis' goal was to strike fear in the hearts of the Third Army. The Nazis' surprise attack and three days of victory under cover of cloud and fog surely would have struck fear in their hearts. But that fear is precisely what God used to bring those same soldiers to the point of total desperation, of total dependence, of turning to Him in prayer because they recognized they had nowhere else to turn. "When I am afraid, I put my trust in You" (Psalm 56:3).

General Patton and the Third Army found themselves in circumstances that may not be all that much different from our circumstances today. It may seem to us as though we are surrounded by enemies on all sides, leaving us feeling helpless and hopeless in our own strength. And that is precisely where He wants us. Only then will we truly seek Him with our whole heart. And He promises that we then will surely find Him (Jeremiah 29:13).

May this story fortify us with courage as we prepare to engage in spiritual warfare to turn the hearts of His people and our nation back to Him.

5

THE PREPARATION

*If My people, who are called by My name, will humble
themselves and pray and seek My face and turn from their wicked
ways, then I will hear from heaven, and I will forgive their sin and
will heal their land.*   II Chronicles 7:14

31 Days of Preparation

Before engaging in battle, warriors are wise to go through some basic
training. We need to understand our purpose, our goal. We need to become
familiar with our defensive armor and our offensive weapons. We need to
know our enemy. But it is even more important to know our Commander
who leads us in battle. Hence these 31 Days of Preparation.

On the following pages, we will find 31 daily assignments. We will be
reading through the entire book of Proverbs together, one chapter each
day. We also will be dissecting a few verses and topics such as fervent prayer
and the armor of God to prepare us for battle.

You may want to grab a journal to write a personal application at the
end of each day's devotion. Taking time to put something in writing helps
us cement that truth in our hearts and minds, and remind us of what we
have learned.

You will find hymn lyrics included at the end of each daily devotion. Having these familiar hymns running in the background of our minds can help keep us focused on Him as we navigate the busyness of each day. If the tune is not familiar, there are multiple renditions online that can facilitate their deep ministry to our souls.

Our daily assignment also includes time to come before our Heavenly Father in prayer with an open heart. Together, we will ask Him to closely examine our hearts, to show us if we are harboring any willful ways and enable us to turn from them. Why? Because we want to be effective warriors in His army. We want to push back the enemy on every front. We want to take back every bit of territory that has been surrendered to the enemy, and then some!

But why are we still focused on II Chronicles 7:14? Because repentance and renewal are both integral and often overlooked ingredients in God's prescription. In fact, this Scripture is so important to our training, we will be spending the first nine days of preparation looking at various aspects of this instructional verse.

Some of us are coming to this project with the idea of just lifting up America, asking God to heal our land. But in these 31 days of preparation, we will see that the healing of our land is only a byproduct. The root problem is not *those* wicked people who won't stop sinning. The root problem lies with *us* if our hearts are not fervently, whole-heartedly seeking after God.

Let's allow the Lord to examine our hearts. Let's turn from our sinful ways. Let's return to the passion of our first love with Him. Let's learn how to "put on the full armor of God" (Ephesians 6:11) and wield our powerful weapons, "made mighty through God to the pulling down of strongholds" (II Corinthians 10:4 KJV).

Since our Lord has laid it on many hearts to pray for spiritual revival in our nation, we invite you to join us in this project. If you want to be an intercessor for our country, now is the time. This is the place. Basic training starts on the following page on December 1.

Let the preparation begin.

The horse is made ready for the day of battle, but victory rests with the Lord.   Proverbs 21:31

December 1   Called

If My people, who are called by My name... II Chronicles 7:14

It may seem obvious, but this is a call to action only for His people. We need to be His, called by His name. What does that mean?

Unfortunately, it doesn't mean if *we* call ourselves Christians. It means if *He* calls us His. Is He our Savior, our Redeemer? Have we accepted His free gift of salvation purchased for us by Jesus?

Let's get real with Him. We can't pretend or hide anything from God Almighty. If we have accepted Jesus as our Savior, has our profession of faith become little more than lip service?

Let's examine our hearts, and see if we aren't counting our "pew warming" or other good deeds to earn us a spot on the team. Have we ever truly come to the end of our "selves" and given up our seat on the throne of our lives? Are we totally committed to His truth, His ways, His plan? Does our faith truly guide our thoughts and actions? Or are we hanging out in the limbo of lukewarm?

Now is the time to get off the fence. Now is the time to truly get right with God Almighty, our Creator, our Redeemer, our Shepherd and Friend.

Let's together take a moment to confirm with Him that He is firmly seated on the throne of our lives and that we are committed to following Him, no matter what. If we have drifted into lukewarm, let's ask Him to make us firmly grounded in His truth and on fire for Him.

Today's Action: Let's read the complete chapter of Proverbs 1 together today, asking Him to let His truth and wisdom sink into our renewed and refreshed hearts. We do not want to be that fool who despises wisdom and instruction.

The fear of the Lord is the beginning of knowledge, but fools despise wisdom and instruction.   Proverbs 1:7

Amazing Grace

Amazing grace-how sweet the sound- That saved a wretch like me! I once was lost but now am found, Was blind but now I see.

'Twas grace that taught my heart to fear, And grace my fears relieved; How precious did that grace appear The hour I first believed!

...will humble themselves... II Chronicles 7:14

After confirming that we are His, the next thing God tells us to do is to humble ourselves. Why?

Think of the most proud person you know. They usually are arrogant. They know it all. They are not teachable. They have all the answers. And if they don't have the answer, they are sure they are smart enough to figure it out on their own. They certainly don't need anyone else to tell them how to live their lives!

What does God say? He says that person is a fool (Proverbs 12:15). Why? Because our ways are foolishness to God; because God's ways are higher than our ways (Isaiah 55:9). His ways are the best ways; they are the right ways; His ways will bring us the most fulfillment.

God's ways may not seem or feel right to us because of our limited understanding. That is why we need to humble ourselves. We need to admit we don't know it all. We need to admit that He is God and we are not. We need to allow ourselves to be taught His ways. And we only can be taught when we are humble.

Let's come in humility before our Almighty and All-Wise, All-Knowing God, admitting that He is God and we are not, that His ways are higher than our ways. Let's ask Him to lead us in His ways.

Today's Action: Let's read every word of the 2nd chapter of Proverbs, asking Him to empty our hearts and minds of pride in our own ways, so we have room to soak up His wisdom and His ways.

Indeed, if you call out for insight and cry aloud for understanding, and if you look for it as for silver and search for it as for hidden treasure, then you will understand the fear of the LORD and find the knowledge of God.   Proverbs 2:3-5

Have Thine Own Way

Have Thine own way, Lord!
Have Thine own way!
Thou art the Potter, I am the clay;
Mold me and make me after Thy will,
While I am waiting, yielded and still.

Have Thine own way, Lord!
Have Thine own way!
Search me and try me, Master, today!
Whiter than snow, Lord, wash me just now,
As in Thy presence humbly I bow.

...and pray... II Chronicles 7:14

After we have confirmed that we are His people and have humbled ourselves before Him, God instructs us to pray. Why?

Immersing ourselves in Proverbs, our faith can feel like nothing more than a long list of *do's* and *don'ts*, mostly *don'ts*. But our Heavenly Father, through Jesus, welcomes us as His children into *relationship*, not religiosity. A vital father-child relationship requires open, two-way communication. He invites us to be in moment-by-moment relationship with Him. That's prayer.

Prayer is simply talking things over with God, much like when we call up a friend and share what's on our heart and mind. We can bring all our concerns to Him, asking for His advice and counsel. (By the way, after taking time to listen, we are wise to follow His advice.)

We can't just dial God up on the phone, so how exactly do we do it? Just start talking. Share our hearts with Him. He already knows what's there. But talking about it helps *us* know what's there.

It's best to start our talk by praising Him for who He is and what He has done. That makes it easier for us to settle our hearts, to be still and know that He is God (Psalm 46:10). Then it is easier to choose to trust Him with our whole heart and not rely on our own understanding (Proverbs 3:5).

Let's humbly come and bow before His Throne, bringing our praise and petitions to Him, recognizing that He alone is God. Let's share our hearts openly with Him so His truth can bring light and life to their every little corner. Then we will be free to simply trust and obey.

Today's Action: Let's read each word of Proverbs 3 together, letting the Lord show us where we may be deceived into seeing ourselves as *wise in our own eyes.*

Do not be wise in your own eyes; fear the LORD and shun evil. This will bring health to your body and nourishment to your bones. Prov. 3:7-8

Trust and Obey

When we walk with the Lord in the light of His Word,
What a glory He sheds on our way!
While we do His good will He abides with us still,
And with all who will trust and obey.

Trust and obey –
For there's no other way
To be happy in Jesus
But to trust and obey.

December 4   Seeking Him

*...and seek my face...*II Chronicles 7:14

After humbling ourselves and praying, the Lord instructs us to seek His face. He just told us to pray; now He says to seek His face. Isn't that the same thing? Yes…and no.

Prayer often ends up being a one-way conversation, where we do all the talking. Most often, we don't even stop to listen to what is on His heart, let alone follow through.

Seeking implies searching, earnestly, with a whole heart. If it is half-hearted, it is not truly seeking. Seeking "His face" implies we are looking to visit with Him personally, to see Him face-to-face and have a one-on-one conversation. And by His amazing plan of prayer, we get to experience that intimate communication at any time we are willing to take the time.

Part of the purpose of dialogue is to understand one another and get on the same page. But let's be honest here. Are we truly seeking God to understand His heart? Do we truly desire to align our lives in agreement with His plans? Or are we just trying to get Him on board with ours?

If we find our prayers being half-hearted, maybe the problem is that we are not open to the input of our *other half,* our unconditionally loving Heavenly Father. Let's earnestly, with a whole heart, seek His face in prayer. Let's listen for His voice, His leading, and then act on how He directs.

Remember His promise that if we seek Him with our whole heart, we will surely find Him, and He will bring us back from our captivity (Jeremiah 29:13-14).

Today's Action: Let's read Proverbs 4 together, not half-heartedly, but with a whole heart, paying attention and listening closely to His wisdom and instruction for us.

My son, pay attention to what I say; turn your ear to my words. Do not let them out of your sight, keep them within your heart; for they are life to those who find them and health to one's whole body.   Prov. 4:20-22

Turn Your Eyes Upon Jesus

O soul, are you weary and troubled?   Turn your eyes upon Jesus,
No light in the darkness you see?   Look full in His wonderful face,
There's light for a look at the Savior,   And the things of earth will grow strangely dim
And life more abundant and free!   In the light of His glory and grace.

December 5   Set Free

...and turn from their wicked ways... II Chronicles 7:14

Why does God instruct us, His people, to first humble ourselves, *then* pray, *then* earnestly seek His face before directing us to turn from our wicked ways? Is it possibly because, without humbling ourselves and praying and earnestly seeking His face, that we, His people who know better, have more difficulty turning from our wicked ways?

Sometimes we who call ourselves Christians can be experts at fooling ourselves. We can have such whitewashed outsides and such filthy insides. And sometimes we are so deceived that we can't even see our own wickedness...or are *unwilling* to see it.

We tend to think that God's judgment is a result of the wickedness of others – those ungodly, sinful people of the world – not us. But this instruction is to *us*. It's *our* wickedness bringing His judgment. Unless we, His people, turn from *our* wicked ways, He will not heal our land.

Have we ever truly repented of our sins, asked for and received forgiveness, and forsaken those sins? We need to ask God Himself, who already knows *all* things, to search our hearts, show us our wicked ways, and enable us to turn from them.

Let's ask God to reveal to us any unbelief, pride or flat-out disobedience that we may not even see lurking in the shadows of our heart and mind. Let's also ask Him to shine His light on any "little" "secret" sins we are trying to hide, so He can enable us to walk away in freedom, once and for all.

Today's Action: Let's read Proverbs 5 together, asking the Lord to help us welcome His discipline and rejoice in His correction, because it alone can keep us from great destruction.

For your ways are in full view of the LORD, and He examines all your paths. The evil deeds of the wicked ensnare them; the cords of their sins hold them fast. For lack of discipline they will die, led astray by their own great folly.   Proverbs 5:21-23

Cleanse Me

Search me, O God, and know my heart today;
Try me, O Savior, know my thoughts, I pray.
See if there be some wicked way in me;
Cleanse me from ev'ry sin and set me free.

19

December 6   Then

...then... II Chronicles 7:14

Then? Yes, just *then*. We are camping out on just this one word today in our 31 days of preparation for battle because it is such a pivotal word.

II Chronicles 7:14 is an "If, then" proposition. If we will, then He will. But the opposite is also true. If we will not, then He will not. If we, His people, will not humble ourselves, pray, seek His face, and turn from our wicked ways, then He will not heal our land.

Do not be deceived. God will not be mocked. He says we will reap what we sow (Galatians 6:7). Just one honest look at our country clearly shows that we, His people, have sown poorly. *We* are called to turn from *our* wicked ways. We truly believe it is His plan to heal our land. But if some of us refuse to turn, God may expose us for the whitewashed-outside, filthy-inside hypocrites we are.

Judgment starts with us, the household of God (I Peter 4:17). This is serious business. Let's voluntarily choose to come to repentance now and avoid the public scandal and tarnishing of His name (as if our current wickedness is not already tarnishing His name). What fools we "wise-in-our-own-eyes" hypocrites can be!

Let's humbly come before our Great Physician and submit our hearts to open heart surgery. Let's let Him examine every chamber, shining His light of truth into every little nook and cranny, so we can be fully restored and healed. Only then will He heal our land.

Today's Action: Let's read Proverbs 6 together, allowing the light of His teachings and the correction of His instruction to guide us to the way of life.

For this command is a lamp, this teaching is a light, and correction and instruction are the way to life. Can a man scoop fire into his lap without his clothes being burned? Can a man walk on hot coals without his feet being scorched?   Proverbs 6:23; 27-28

Just As I Am

Just as I am without one plea
But that Thy blood was shed for me,
And that Thou bidd'st me come to Thee,
O Lamb of God, I come! I come!

Just as I am, and waiting not
To rid my soul of one dark blot,
To Thee whose blood can cleanse each spot,
O Lamb of God, I come! I come!

December 7   Wholly His

*...I will hear from heaven...*II Chronicles 7:14

After we humble ourselves, pray, seek His face, *and* turn from our wicked ways, the Lord of Hosts says He will hear from heaven. What does He hear? Psalm 102:19-20 tells us that He looks down from His sanctuary in heaven and *intently* searches the earth in order to hear the prisoner's sigh. Even a simple sigh. He listens for our sighs, our dependent cries, and promises to hear from heaven. How amazing is our God!

Yet, while we stand amazed that He searches out even a sigh, we somehow think He doesn't really see what we don't want Him to see. How ludicrous to think we can get away with the "secret" sins we harbor in the recesses of our hearts.

Proverbs is packed with warning about falling prey to sin, particularly sexual sin. Why such a focus? Is it because it often begins almost imperceptibly and then suddenly is in full bloom? Or because we think it's just "our little secret" that no one else knows about? Fools are we, thinking we can fool God!

"Choose you this day whom you will serve" (Joshua 24:15). Will you choose to turn to God and truly give up your "hidden" sin? Or will you choose to turn away because, like Gollum in Tolkien's *Lord of the Rings*, you are unwilling to give up *My Precious*, your "secret" sin?

Let's humbly come before our all-knowing God and King, asking Him again to search our hearts. If we have not already done so, let's ask Him to help us to truly, once and for all, let go of our "little" "secret" sins.

Today's Action: Let's read chapter 7 of Proverbs together, choosing to apply His direct, but loving, words of warning to our hearts so that we might not sin against Him.

With persuasive words she led him astray; she seduced him with her smooth talk. All at once he followed her like an ox going to the slaughter, like a deer stepping into a noose 'til an arrow pierces his liver, like a bird darting into a snare, little knowing it will cost him his life. Proverbs 7:21-23

Breathe on Me, Breath of God

Breathe on me, Breath of God,	Breathe on me, Breath of God,
Fill me with life anew,	'Til I am wholly Thine,
That I may love what Thou dost love	'Til all this earthly part of me
And do what Thou wouldst do.	Glows with Thy fire divine.

December 8   Forgiven

*...and I will forgive their sin...*II Chronicles 7:14

We are into the 8th day of preparation and we still haven't gotten to the "heal our land" part! Why did God first say that He will forgive our sins before He says that He will heal our land?

To reinforce the truth. The truth is that we need to turn from our wicked ways and receive forgiveness before He will heal our land.

We probably want our land healed so we don't have to experience discomfort. We don't like being mocked for our convictions, nor the idea of being persecuted for our faith. We fear that the persecution of Christians around the globe may be headed to our shores. We just want our old comfortable life back, with its blissful ignorance and/or tolerance of sin.

But God is deadly serious about sin, even if we are not. Why else would He come down to earth to live a perfect life and die an unimaginably painful, excruciating death if sin wasn't such a matter of life and death for all eternity?

We are seeking a happier life; but God is after a *holier* life. Let's double down on our commitment to choose a holier life, in line with His Word. Only then can we experience a truly happy, joyful life.

Let's humbly approach the Throne of Grace today, rejoicing in His grace that offers us forgiveness of our sin through the substitutionary death of Jesus on the cross. Let's revel in the fact that "as far as the east is from the west," that is how far He has removed our sins from us (Psalm 103:12). Having been saved from the eternal penalty of our sin, let us now seek to know and do His will.

Today's Action: Together let's read Proverbs 8, choosing to value His words of wisdom and instruction over anything else in this world, letting them penetrate and change our willful hearts.

Choose my instruction instead of silver, knowledge rather than choice gold, for wisdom is more precious than rubies, and nothing you desire can compare with her.   Proverbs 8:10-11

I'd Rather Have Jesus

I'd rather have Jesus than silver or gold,	Than to be the king of a vast domain,
I'd rather be His than have riches untold;	And be held in sin's dread sway;
I'd rather have Jesus than houses or land,	I'd rather have Jesus than anything
Yes, I'd rather be led by His nail-pierced hand,	This world affords today.

...and will heal their land. II Chronicles 7:14

Well, finally, we are getting to the point that we thought we were looking for in the first place – healing our land! We tend to think healing our land is the end game. We do want our land healed, but what does that look like? Is it a return to *normal*, a return to *the good life*, not having to worry about our bank accounts shrinking, our comforts or our security threatened? If so, we are focused on the *stuff* of life, not the *substance* of life.

We must not expect that if God heals our land, life will go back to the way we were. Why? Because the way we were was not God-honoring. We were lost in lukewarm, acting blissfully ignorant, or complacently tolerant, of sin. Why would God answer our fervent prayers by returning us to *that* state? That is what got us in trouble in the first place. He has much more in mind. Renewal. Restoration. Revival.

The most essential and life-changing result of our intercession would be the cleansing and healing of our hearts. The healing of our land is only a side benefit, a symptom and sign of a healing of His people.

Imagine revival! Imagine how our world could change if His truth controlled our hearts and minds. Walking in integrity, our compassionate hearts would focus our energies and resources to be the hands and feet of Jesus worldwide. We would stand up for persecuted Christians, both here and abroad. We would be filled with an urgency to spread the Good News, to fulfill the Great Commission. We would see not only a healing of our land, but a healing of our world!

Let's praise the Lord for the opportunity to turn from our wicked ways and receive forgiveness; let's ask Him to heal our hearts so we can be used by Him to bring healing to our land and our world.

Today's Action: Let's read Proverbs 9 together, taking the time to let its wisdom and correction change our hearts and our lives, so we can live a long and fruitful life for Him and His purposes.

For through Me your days will be many, and years will be added to your life.   Proverbs 9:11

Channels Only

How I praise Thee, precious Savior!
That Thy love laid hold of me;
Thou hast saved and cleansed and filled me,
That I might Thy channel be.

Channels only, Blessed Master -
But with all Thy wondrous pow'r
Flowing thru us, Thou canst use us
Ev'ry day and ev'ry hour.

December 10   Fervent

The fervent prayer of a righteous man avails much. James 5:16 KJV

As we prepare to be effective intercessors, we certainly would want to know how to pray prayers that *avail much*. This verse indicates that our prayers need to be fervent. But what does it mean to pray fervently?

The word "fervent" has been defined as "passionate; heartfelt; wholehearted". Those descriptions help us realize that fervent prayer is not a matter of the words, the style or the length. It's a matter of the heart, a whole heart. The many words of a "chattering fool" are powerless because their goal is to impress, not to implore with a whole heart.

"Fervent" is the opposite of "half-hearted." A half-hearted prayer, even of a righteous man, does not avail much. We need to believe with all our hearts that He alone has the power to convict; He alone has the power to save; He alone has the power to restore.

James doesn't give us any more detail defining or describing fervent prayer. There isn't a to-do list like "Set your alarm to go off every hour and then pray, totally focused, for five minutes every hour for ten days." Wouldn't we like a description like that? Then we could feel like we had met the mark. We had achieved. We had accomplished. Given a specific 5-step program, we would do the five steps and then be proud of *our* accomplishment. We would lose sight of our need for a moment-by-moment dependence on Him. We need Him every moment to guide us in our prayers so we stay in line with His will and His kingdom purposes.

Let's fervently seek His face so we can be on the same page as our Commander, seeking His will and accepting His commands to turn from our wicked ways so we can walk in wisdom and integrity.

Today's Action: Let's read Proverbs 10 together, asking Him to direct us in the way of the wise, keeping us from the way of the wicked and the folly of the fool.

The wise in heart accepts commands, but a chattering fool comes to ruin.   Proverbs 10:8

Teach Me Thy Way

Teach me Thy Way, O Lord,	Help me to walk aright,
Teach me Thy Way!	More by faith, less by sight;
Thy guiding grace afford -	Lead me with heav'nly light -
Teach me Thy Way!	Teach me Thy Way!

December 11   Only His Righteousness

...a righteous man... James 5:16 KJV

Yesterday, we looked at "fervent prayer". The next phrase in James 5 says that it is a righteous man's fervent prayer that avails much. What is meant by a "righteous" man? (Let's first clarify that the word "man" is generic, as in mankind, and includes both men and women.)

We can all be thankful James uses the word "righteous" and not *perfect*, because there is no way we could ever qualify as *perfect* sons and daughters. Isaiah graphically reminds us that even what we think of as our "righteousnesses" are as filthy rags! (Isaiah 64:6 KJV) It is impossible to be seen as righteous by God based on any goodness of our own. But since we have accepted the gift of faith and salvation that Jesus purchased for us, we can now be seen by God as righteous. When we approach God in prayer, we are clothed in the righteousness of Jesus. What a reassuring image!

But Psalm 66:18 tells us that sin hinders our prayers. And I John 1:8-9 says "If we claim to be without sin, we deceive ourselves, and the truth is not in us." However, "If we confess our sins, He is faithful and just and will forgive us our sins, and purify us from all unrighteousness."

Acknowledging that we do have sin, confessing it and receiving forgiveness from Him are each necessary steps before we can move forward with a cleansed heart and renewed spirit. So, like David, let's ask God to "Create in me a pure heart, O God, and renew a steadfast spirit within me" (Psalm 51:10). Let's come confidently before the Throne of Grace (Hebrews 4:16) with thanksgiving to Jesus for purchasing our "robe of righteousness". Let's ask Him to show us how we may be soiling that white robe, and ask Him to enable us to walk blameless before Him.

Today's Action: Let's read Proverbs 11 together, letting these words of wisdom fall on good ground and take root, bearing much fruit for Him.

The truly righteous attain life, but whoever pursues evil finds death. The fruit of the righteous is a tree of life, and the one who wins souls is wise.   Proverbs 11:19, 30

Nothing But the Blood

What can wash away my sin?	Oh, precious is the flow
Nothing but the blood of Jesus;	That makes me white as snow;
What can make me whole again?	No other fount I know,
Nothing but the blood of Jesus.	Nothing but the blood of Jesus.

December 12   Empowered

...avails much. James 5:16 KJV

After confessing our sins, receiving a cleansed heart and renewed spirit, and praying fervently, what results can we expect? What does it mean to *avail much?*

In II Corinthians 10:4-5, Paul declares "For the weapons of our warfare are not carnal, but mighty through God to the pulling down of strongholds; casting down imaginations, and every high thing that exalteth itself against the knowledge of God."(KJV) What magnificent, powerful weaponry!

What are these weapons that are "not carnal, but mighty through God"? Prayer and the Word are the mighty weapons we have been given. Thankfully, their might is not dependent on the expert way in which we wield them. They are only mighty through God Almighty!

Our prayers can pull down strongholds in His people and our nation, as well as arguments that exalt themselves "against the knowledge of God." We may not know exactly what these strongholds and imaginations are, but God Almighty knows. And these are precisely what our mighty weapons were made to take on! Through God, we can expect them to accomplish much!

We have been called to this specific action at this specific time because our Good Shepherd is on the move, seeking out His sheep who have gone astray. How exciting it is that He has given us the privilege of partnering with Him through prayer to restore the hearts and lives of His people! If we, clothed in the righteousness of Jesus, pray fervently, we can enter this battle knowing that our prayers will *avail much.* Let us joyfully come before Him, rejoicing that He has invited us to partner with Him to revive His people. May He use our tongues to bring His healing.

Today's Action: Let's read Proverbs 12 together, asking Him to soften our hearts to receive His wisdom so we bring healing with our prayers.

The words of the reckless pierce like swords, but the tongue of the wise brings healing.   Proverbs 12:18

Sweet Hour of Prayer

Sweet hour of prayer, sweet hour of prayer,	In seasons of distress and grief
That calls me from a world of care	My soul has often found relief,
And bids me at my Father's throne	And oft escaped the tempter's snare
Make all my wants and wishes known!	By thy return, sweet hour of prayer.

December 13   Battle Ready

*Put on the full armor of God, so that you can take your stand
against the devil's schemes.*   Ephesians 6:11

Let's be careful not to take this on too lightly. This is war! Our enemy is
deadly serious about this war for the hearts and souls of God's people and
our nation. So should we.

We are joining together in a spiritual battle. We have declared war, so
we should expect opposition. It is beyond foolish to think Satan is just
going to walk away without a fight.

We have been given a suit of armor so we can stand firm in this fight.
Ephesians 6:12-13 says we fight "not against flesh and blood, but against
the rulers, against the authorities, against the powers of this dark world and
against the spiritual forces of evil in the heavenly realms. Therefore put on
the full armor of God, so that when the day of evil comes, you may be able
to stand your ground."

We are told to put on the whole armor of God so we can stand against
the deceptions, tricks, and schemes of the devil. And we are wise to respect
and follow that instruction.

Over the next few days, we will examine each piece of our armor so we
can stand firm in our fight against the enemy and his forces of evil who
have been unleased on and in our nation. Sound scary? Only if we were
going it alone and in our own strength. But we are fighting in the power of
His might, with the victory already assured because of Jesus!

Let's come before His throne together today, thankful for all the many
truths He has given us in His Word that allow us to take a victorious stand
against the enemy and his evil forces.

Today's Action: Let's read Proverbs 13 together, with a heart full of
faith and commitment to be wise by following our Father's instructions to
get ready for battle.

*Whoever scorns instruction will pay for it, but whoever respects a
command is rewarded.*   Proverbs 13:13

Soldiers of Christ, Arise

Soldiers of Christ, arise	Strong in the Lord of Hosts
And put your armor on,	And in His mighty pow'r
Strong in the strength which God supplies	Who in the strength of Jesus trusts
Thru His eternal Son;	Is more than conqueror.

*Stand firm then, with the belt of truth buckled around your
waist...*   Ephesians 6:14

The purpose of putting on God's armor is so we can stand against the schemes and deceptions of the enemy. Therefore, it's most important to start by arming ourselves with God's truth. Only *His* truth can expose and destroy the enemy's deceptions.

In the Roman soldiers' suit of armor, the first thing they put on was their belt. Then they would tuck the end of their tunic up under their belt. This immediately increased their mobility by freeing their legs from being tripped up by their clothing.[viii] If attacked by the enemy before they could get their hands on any other gear, the belt would at least allow them to run to safety if necessary. That's one reason our belt is listed first in our armor.

But why a belt of truth? Have you heard the phrase "gird your loins"? It means to prepare for action. If we gird our loins with His truth, it is easier to identify the opposite - the lies with which Satan tries to trip us up.

To be girded with truth, we first need to know *The Truth*, our Lord and Savior, Jesus Christ (John 14:6). Then, because God's Word is truth (John 17:17), we need to be firmly grounded in His Word, totally committed to who He is, to what He has said, and to what He can do.

Let's ask our God to help us securely buckle our belt of truth today. Let's remind Him and ourselves of some of that truth: that He alone is God Almighty; He alone hears and answers prayer; He alone knows the beginning from the end; He alone works all things together for the good of those who love Him. These truths are a great way to set our minds to battle.

Today's Action: Let's read Proverbs 14 together, and ask Him to show us any ways that may seem right to us, but actually are the devil's deadly lies and deceptions poisoning our hearts and minds. Then let's commit to stand firmly in the truth.

*There is a way that appears to be right, but in the end it leads to
death.*   Proverbs 14:12

Standing on the Promises

Standing on the promises of Christ my King,	Standing, standing,
Thru eternal ages let His praises ring;	Standing on the promises of God my Savior;
"Glory in the highest" I will shout and sing,	Standing, standing,
Standing on the promises of God.	I'm standing on the promises of God.

December 15   Breastplate of Righteousness

*...with the breastplate of righteousness in place...*Ephesians 6:14

After our belt of truth is secure, we can ask ourselves "What's our most vulnerable place?" It's our heart. That's why the breastplate is our second piece of armor we put on.

What is our "breastplate of righteousness"? Thankfully, it is not a breastplate of our own righteousness, which Isaiah describes as filthy rags (Isaiah 64:6). Through faith, our breastplate is made of the righteousness of Jesus (II Corinthians 5:21).

The Roman soldier's breastplate was made of bronze or chain mail and had loops or buckles that attached it to the belt, both front and back. The weight was then carried by the belt and not the soldier's shoulders.[ix] Our shoulders don't have to carry the weight of providing our righteousness. We can rest in the perfect provision of His.

In Philippians 3:9, Paul said he wanted to "be found in Him, not having a righteousness of my own that comes from the law, but that which is through faith in Christ – the righteousness that comes from God and is by faith." An online writer for gotquestions.org put it this way: "The breastplate of righteousness has Christ's name stamped on it, as though He said, 'Your righteousness isn't sufficient to protect you. Wear mine.' "[x]

Let's thank Jesus for providing us His breastplate of righteousness to protect our hearts, and ask Him to expose anything in our lives that might mar His perfect breastplate. Then let's confess, repent and be cleansed so that no sin tarnishes this costly, beautiful breastplate He has given us.

Today's action: Let's read Proverbs 15 together, letting this chapter's words shine a light into our open, redeemed hearts so our prayers will be pleasing to Him.

The LORD detests the sacrifice of the wicked, but the prayer of the upright pleases Him. The LORD is far from the wicked, but He hears the prayer of the righteous.   Proverbs 15:8, 29

My Jesus, I Love Thee

My Jesus, I love Thee!   My gracious Redeemer,
I know Thou are mine -   My Savior art Thou;
For Thee all the follies –   If ever I loved Thee,
Of sin I resign;   My Jesus, 'tis now.

December 16   "Good News Shoes"

...with your feet fitted with the readiness that comes from the gospel of peace.   Ephesians 6:15

"Feet fitted with the readiness that comes from the gospel of peace" is a phrase that doesn't make much sense at first. So let's break it down a bit.

The Roman soldiers' feet were "fitted" with military-grade sandals. Straps were attached to the sole which crisscrossed the foot and then tied up around the ankle. This created a secure sole, which was spiked to give a firm grip on slippery terrain. This footwear helped them not only hold their ground, but more easily gain ground when called to advance in battle. In the same way, our "good news shoes" can help us stand firm as well as advance against our enemy.

The phrase "with the readiness" is similar to II Timothy 4:2 and I Peter 3:15, where we are told to be ready at all times, both in and out of season, to share the *good news* of the hope that is in us. We should have the *good news* of peace with God always front and center. This constant focus will strengthen us with firm conviction as we do battle.

The "gospel of peace" is the *good news* that we can have reconciliation and peace with God through Jesus' death and resurrection. This peace with God is secure through all eternity, and through all of life's *unpeaceful* circumstances. Now that's good news!

Let's thank the Lord that no matter how much of our world gives way, He has everything under control. His plan cannot be thwarted by the enemy. Let's lace up our "good news shoes" so we will always have a readiness to share His *good news.* But let's also stop to seek His wisdom and His direction about how, when and what to speak into another person's life. He will give us the words.

Today's Action: Let's read Proverbs 16 together, with a heart thirsty for His words of wisdom, His words to speak into the lives of others.

To humans belong the plans of the heart, but from the LORD comes the proper answer of the tongue.   Proverbs 16:1

I Love to Tell the Story

I love to tell the story of unseen things above,
Of Jesus and His glory, of Jesus and His love;
I love to tell the story because I know 'tis true,
It satisfies my longings as nothing else can do.

I love to tell the story!
'Twill be my theme in glory –
To tell the old, old story
Of Jesus and His love.

December 17   Shield of Faith

In addition to all this, take up the shield of faith, with which you can extinguish all the flaming arrows of the evil one.   Ephesians 6:16

The Roman soldier's shield was intentionally large. It was designed so the soldier could crouch down and hide behind it, if necessary. Groups of soldiers could also gather together and put their shields above and around themselves, forming a "tortoise shell" of protection.

Our shield of faith can give us a place of refuge, a place of protection, a place of rest. When things are looking out of control, our faith confirms that *none* of this is a surprise to our God. He is still on His throne, and He *will* accomplish His will, for our good and for the furthering of His purposes.

Paul also describes our shield of faith as an effective fire extinguisher, quenching "all the flaming arrows of the evil one." Flaming arrows were the most powerful weapons of Roman warfare. So a wise soldier would soak his shield before battle to keep fiery darts from setting it on fire.

In the same way, we are wise to keep our hearts and minds soaked in the living water of the Word. Then our shield of faith can extinguish *all* of our enemy's flaming arrows. Our enemy may think his fiery darts of doubt, fear or temptation are powerful. But our Word-soaked faith is greater still.

Our weapons of warfare are too powerful for our enemy and he knows it! If only we knew it! He only wins if we get distracted, lay down our weapons, or if we never even enter the fight. So let's fight! Victory is ours! After all, faith is the victory that overcomes the world! (I John 5:4)

Today's Action: Let's read Proverbs 17 together, asking Him to help us see life's circumstances through our eyes of faith, which can give us a cheerful heart and protect us from a crushed spirit.

A cheerful heart is good medicine, but a crushed spirit dries up the bones.   Proverbs 17:22

Faith is the Victory!

Encamped along the hills of light,   Against the foe in vales below
Ye Christian soldiers, rise;   Let all our strength be hurled;
And press the battle ere the night   Faith is the victory, we know
Shall veil the glowing skies.   That overcomes the world.

Faith is the victory! Faith is the victory!
O glorious victory that overcomes the world!

31

December 18   Helmet of Salvation

*Take the helmet of salvation...*Ephesians 6:17

The purpose of a helmet is to protect a soldier's head. But in this metaphor, our helmet of salvation is issued to protect our minds. While our breastplate of righteousness specifically protects our hearts, our helmet of salvation specifically protects our minds.

How does salvation protect our minds? Our salvation gives us reconciliation, peace with God. Philippians 4:7 says "And the peace of God, which transcends all understanding, will guard your hearts and your minds in Christ Jesus." The peace of God protects our minds. Our minds can be at rest in the midst of any circumstance because our salvation is a done deal; it's an accomplished fact; our peace with God is secure for all eternity.

Referring to His sheep, Jesus said "I give them eternal life, and they shall never perish; no one will snatch them out of My hand" (John 10:28). As His sheep who hear and follow His voice, our redemption, our salvation, is secure forever. May we stand amazed that He has chosen us; that He has redeemed us; that no man can pluck us out of His hand! May this assurance protect our minds as we prepare to engage in battle with the great deceiver. Because of our salvation through the substitutionary death and resurrection of Jesus Christ, our ultimate victory is assured!

Let's come into His presence today, thankful that we have been issued a helmet of salvation to guard our minds. Let's ask Him to help us keep our minds sharp, being sober and watchful, because our enemy is always on the prowl looking for moments of weakness (1 Peter 5:8). Let's ask God to confirm to us the security and surety of our salvation, and then use that as a reference point to expose our enemy's deceptions and clever schemes.

Today's Action: Let's read Proverbs 18 together, committed to challenging the great deceiver's deceptions, exposing his lies in our lives so we can walk in integrity and truth.

The first to present his case seems right, 'til another comes forward and questions him.   Proverbs 18:17

My Savior's Love

I stand amazed in the presence	How marvelous! How wonderful!
Of Jesus the Nazarene,	And my song shall ever be:
And wonder how He could love me,	How marvelous! How wonderful
A sinner, condemned, unclean.	Is my Savior's love for me!

December 19   The Sword

...and the sword of the Spirit, which is the Word of God. Eph. 6:17

Today, let's look at our last physical piece of armor, our sword, which is clearly defined as the Word of God. This image is repeated again in Hebrews 4:12 - "For the Word of God is alive and active. Sharper than any double-edged sword, it penetrates even to dividing soul and spirit, joints and marrow; it judges the thoughts and attitudes of the heart."
Sharper than a double-edged sword! That's powerful! But out of our six physical pieces of armor – our belt, breastplate, shoes, shield, helmet, and sword - the sword is the only piece that can be used for offense. The rest of our armor is for defense. This tells us God takes our protection seriously, so *we* should take our protection seriously. It has been provided to us, so we are foolish not to use it. Why? Because our adversary the devil "prowls around like a roaring lion looking for someone to devour" (I Peter 5:8).

We would also be well-advised to follow Jesus' example when He effectively fought Satan's temptations in the wilderness. As described in Matthew 4 and Luke 4, Jesus responded to each of Satan's temptations with "It is written...", quoting the Word. God Himself quoted the Word, who could have destroyed Satan with just one breath! How much more should we value His Word, our powerful weapon of the sword of truth.

Interestingly, the ever-clever Satan took note and quoted scripture in the last of his temptations, so he is also aware of the Word. We shouldn't be surprised then when the Word gets misquoted and misapplied. It is all part of our adversary's clever schemes. All the more reason to keep our swords sharpened by diligent, deep study of God's Holy Word. Let's thank the Lord for giving us the powerful weapon of His Word, and ask Him to create an insatiable hunger and thirst for more of it in our daily lives. May we see it as our only source of truth to counter our adversary's lies.

Today's Action: Let's read Proverbs 19 together with a teachable spirit, willing to receive and apply the instruction and correction it offers.

Stop listening to instruction, my son, and you will stray from the words of knowledge.   Proverbs 19:27

Holy Bible, Book Divine

Holy Bible, book divine, precious treasure, thou art mine;
Mine to tell me whence I came,
Mine to teach me what I am.

33

And pray in the Spirit on all occasions with all kinds of prayers and requests...be alert and always keep on praying...   Ephesians 6:18

Paul ends his discourse on the armor of God with the words "and pray...on all occasions...with all kinds of prayers and requests...and always keep on praying...". It is reasonable to suggest that our sword (the Word) and prayer are our two offensive pieces of armor.

Paul describes our weapons as "not carnal, but mighty through God for the pulling down of strongholds" (II Corinthians 10:4 KJV). Pulling down strongholds! Sounds like mighty powerful weapons we are given!

But what makes our prayers powerful? The length of time or the words we say? No. Our prayers are only mighty "through God". He takes our prayers and petitions and empowers them with His power, His authority, His might. Our prayers are powerful not because of *how*, but *to whom*, we pray. That lifts a lot of the performance pressure from us. We just need to be faithful to pray as He directs. And we know He will be faithful to answer – in His time, in His way, and in His plan.

Let's also keep in mind that the purpose of prayer is not to *change* the will of God; it is to *accomplish* the will of God. Therefore, we need to be frequently checking in with headquarters to make sure we are on the same page as our Commander. We need to seek His face, listening for His direction as He gives us advice and guidance to effectively wage this war.

Let's approach the Throne of Grace today, thankful for the mind-blowing fact that we can talk one-on-one with the God of the Universe. We have the privilege of seeking His face, receiving His advice and guidance for effective warfare in order to advance.

Today's Action: Let's intently read every word of Proverbs 20, with a focus to search out and apply those corrections and instructions that are most needed in our own lives.

Plans are established by seeking advice; so if you wage war, obtain guidance.   Proverbs 20:18

What a Friend We Have in Jesus

What a friend we have in Jesus,
All our sins and griefs to bear!
What a privilege to carry
Everything to God in prayer!

O what peace we often forfeit,
O what needless pain we bear,
All because we do not carry
Everything to God in prayer!

December 21   Wielding our Weapons

The weapons we fight with are not the weapons of the world. On the contrary, they have divine power to demolish strongholds.   II Cor. 10:4

We have been given two weapons that not only protect us defensively from our enemy's attacks, but they can also be used offensively "for the tearing down of strongholds" (KJV). These two weapons are prayer and our sword - God's Word.

Why is prayer considered one of our weapons? It's not in the armor list, is it? Well, it actually is, but not as an actual piece of armor you put on. It is a weapon that we use along with our sword. After instructing us to put on all the various pieces of armor, including "the sword of the Spirit, which is the word of God", Paul continues with this instruction: "...and pray...on all occasions...with all kinds of prayers and requests" (Ephesians 6:18). Clearly, prayer is an essential part of our arsenal.

How do we wield our weapons of prayer and our sword, the Word? They actually work very well together. Our prayers can include praying His Word to Him, recounting His promises; reaffirming His truth. This not only reminds us to pray according to His will, but it also strengthens our faith because we end up reminding ourselves of His truth in the process.

What can that look like? We can, for example, declare that He promised that His Word will not return void (Isaiah 55:11); we can ask Him to give His people a pure heart and renew a right spirit in us (Psalm 51:10); we can pray that, as Lord of the harvest, He would send reapers (Matthew 9:38).

He has promised to lead, if we will ask and then heed. Let's ask the Lord today to help us learn to effectively wield our weapons of prayer and the Word, listening to His leading and direction in this battle. He knows what strongholds we should pray against so His forces can destroy them.

Today's Action: With a humble and teachable heart, let's together read Proverbs 21, asking Him to reveal strongholds He wants to demolish.

One who is wise can go up against the city of the mighty and pull down the stronghold in which they trust.   Proverbs 21:22

Lead On, O King Eternal

Lead on, O King Eternal, the day of march has come!
Henceforth in fields of conquest Thy tents shall be our home;
Thru days of preparation Thy grace has made us strong,
And now, O King Eternal, we lift our battle song.

35

December 22   Suit Up!

How foolish we would be to learn all about our armor and then just admire it. We are instructed to put it on. We are in a battle, so we need to suit up! But how do we do that? Paul doesn't say exactly how we put it on.

It's probably not important *how* we put it on; it's important *that* we put it on. We can thank the Lord every morning for each piece as we visualize them, for example, asking His help to use them as He leads. Or we can say "I put on my belt of truth", and then thank Him for each piece. We can remind ourselves at any time of day or night about each amazing piece of our armor, asking Him to make sure that our "belt of truth" is securely buckled, that He will show us anything that we are thinking or doing that might tarnish His "breastplate of righteousness", etc.

Hand motions help to remember what the pieces of our armor are. The first three – our belt, breastplate and shoes – require two hands to put on, so those go on first – hands on hips for belt, on chest for breastplate, then point to our feet to "put on" our shoes. Then "pick up" our shield with our left hand, "put on" our helmet with our right hand, then use our now-free right hand to "pick up" our sword. Now, with prayer, we are fully armed and battle-ready!

A prudent person recognizes danger and prepares for it. So let's make sure we are fully protected in our amazing suit of God's armor at all times. The most important thing to remember about each piece of armor is that each one is grounded in His Word. So let's make sure our ideas about truth, righteousness, the gospel, faith, and salvation continue to line up with His Word. And when we feel particularly under attack, let's immerse ourselves all that much more in His Word. Then let's thank Him for His provision and the privilege of joining in His battle to accomplish His will.

Today's Action: Let's read Proverbs 22 together, with hearts that seek His correction and direction, so we can be more effective warriors.

The prudent see danger and take refuge, but the simple keep going and pay the penalty.   Proverbs 22:3

Onward, Christian Soldiers

Onward, Christian soldiers, marching as to war,
With the cross of Jesus going on before!
Christ, the royal Master, leads against the foe;
Forward into battle see His banner go!
Onward, Christian soldiers, marching as to war, With the cross of Jesus going on before!

December 23   The Dart of Doubt

Paul says our shield of faith effectively extinguishes Satan's fiery darts, so let's talk about one of his most effective darts – doubt. It worked with Eve when Satan asked her "Did God *really* say…?" (Genesis 3:1). If only she had responded with truth, we wouldn't be in such a world of trouble!

When Satan tries to distract us with doubt, one of the best extinguishing truths is "In the beginning God…"(Genesis 1:1). When doubt tries to creep in, counter with the creation. Go outside and look at the stars. There are so many stars, we don't even know just how many there are. Yet the Word says He calls them all by name. It takes our breath away. That could not have just happened by chance. There has to be a God!

If it's daytime, examine the unbelievable intricacies of nature. Watch the tiny ants as they scurry about, touching their antennae as they communicate some kind of message and hurry on their way. Or watch a spider become aware of your presence and race off to find the nearest hiding place. How can there be "thinking" skills in such tiny little creatures? There has to be a Creator!

Or re-read the account of how God rescued the Israelites out of Egypt (Exodus 7-14). This account was written by Moses who actually witnessed, first hand, those amazing signs and wonders! They really happened! There has to be a God who created and is intimately involved with His creation. That same God is the same yesterday, today, and forever (Hebrews 13:8).

Let's remind ourselves of His truths that are especially meaningful to each of us. Grounded in the truth of His Word, let's gird our loins, prepared to stand firm in this, His battle. Let's ask Him to help us detect and douse those fiery darts of doubt. Then let's pray confidently in renewed faith, knowing our prayers have been answered even if we don't ever get to see it, because we walk by faith and not by sight (II Corinthians 5:7).

Today's Action: Let's read Proverbs 23 together, turning our back on doubt, and choosing to apply His instruction to our hearts and minds today.

Apply your heart to instruction and your ears to words of knowledge.
                                                              Proverbs 23:12

Count Your Blessings

When upon life's billows you are tempest-tossed,
When you are discouraged, thinking all is lost,
Count your many blessings – name them one by one,
And it will surprise you what the Lord hath done.

Communication. It can be one of the greatest challenges of life. Often communication can turn into a verbal competition instead. We end up talking *at* each other instead of *with* each other.

Visualize a triangle. When two people are across from each other on the bottom line of that triangle trying to communicate, it can become a "boxing match". While a gentle answer can turn away wrath (Proverbs 15:1), conflict can remain because it is less about the topic and more a matter of the heart. That's where prayer comes in. Only God can change hearts. Visualize God at the top of the triangle. We can send our concerns up the triangle to God, and ask Him to work down the sides of the triangle to work the necessary change in our hearts. Once we ask God to handle it, we can let it go. Our lives can be less stressed, as we choose to trust God.

The visual of a triangle can also help demonstrate the power of prayer. The power of prayer is not found in the prayers we send up to God; it is only found in His powerful answers coming back down. That's why Paul can say that the weapons of our warfare are "mighty *through God* to the pulling down of strongholds" (II Corinthians 10:4 KJV – emphasis added).

This triangle concept is also consistent with Jesus' teaching in Matthew 9:37-38: "The harvest is plentiful but the workers are few. Ask the Lord of the harvest, therefore, to send out workers into His harvest field." He didn't tell us to go make others work the harvest. That could end up in fisticuffs. Or we could end up trying to do it in our own power. Instead, Jesus says to pray that the *Lord* would send workers. Our role is to pray; His role is to call, equip and send. We may be the reapers that He sends, but the sending is up to Him. So let's come before Him, asking Him to bring the hearts of His people and our nation back to Him, and then follow His guidance for what He wants *us* to do as He sends us into battle for His purposes.

Today's Action: Let's read Proverbs 24 together, seeking guidance so that we can help bring about the victorious harvest He has planned.

Surely you need guidance to wage war, and victory is won through many advisers.   Proverbs 24:6

Bring Them In

Hark! 'Tis the Shepherd's voice I hear,	Bring them in, bring them in,
Out in the desert dark and drear,	Bring them in from the fields of sin;
Calling the sheep who've gone astray	Bring them in, bring them in,
Far from the Shepherd's fold away.	Bring the wand'ring ones to Jesus.

December 25   Yielding

The LORD is my strength and my shield; my heart trusts in Him,
and He helps me. My heart leaps for joy, and with my song I praise
Him.   Psalm 28:7

This verse makes an excellent framework for prayer. If we start by recognizing that He alone is our strength and shield, we can more easily yield our spirit to His control to be used for His purposes. We can more readily accept that His ways are higher than our ways. We can more easily focus our hearts on having Him alone be our heart's desire.

It's so natural for us to have the focus on ourselves, isn't it? After all, our individual minds are being carried around inside our individual bodies 24-7! We are inclined to think about ourselves all the time, constantly checking in on ourselves. "How do I feel? Am I hungry or thirsty? Am I too hot or too cold? Do I feel loved, appreciated, valued?" We sometimes think that only after we check the boxes that all is fine in *our* world, then we might have some time leftover to give to God or to others.

In contrast, this Psalm directs us to speak truth to our *self,* who naturally is *self*-ish and *self*-focused. The truth reminds our *self* that we are not our own strength; we are not our own shield. We are wise to yield our spirits to Him alone, to trust in Him alone. We can turn our focus from ourselves and make Him and His kingdom the focus of our hearts. Then, and only then, can our hearts be emptied of *self* and be filled with His joy, with His love. And then we will long to praise and worship Him alone.

This is Christmas Day. Let's bow in humble worship to the King of kings. May we rededicate our lives for His use, asking Him to remove the dross from the silver so we can be useful vessels for Him in His kingdom plans and purposes.

Today's Action: Let's read Proverbs 25 together, submitting to His refining fire, so we can be used to bring more honor and glory to Him.

Remove the dross from the silver, and a silversmith can produce a
vessel.   Proverbs 25:4

O Come All Ye Faithful

O come, all ye faithful, joyful and triumphant,	O come, let us adore Him,
Come ye, O come ye to Bethlehem;	O come, let us adore Him,
Come and behold Him,	O come, let us adore Him,
Born the King of angels:	Christ, the Lord.

December 26   Blind Spot

Search me, God, and know my heart...see if there is any offensive way in me, and lead me in the way everlasting.   Psalm 139:23-24

If we have spent any time behind the wheel of a car, we all have experienced the shock of the "Blind Spot". How is it possible that an entire vehicle can be hidden from our view? And what devastating consequences for us and others if we ignore its reality!

The same can be true in our own lives. Jesus asks us in Matthew 7:3 - "Why do you look at the speck of sawdust in your brother's eye and pay no attention to the plank in your own eye?" Talk about a blind spot!

None of us wants to be called a hypocrite. But that is precisely the word that Jesus uses to describe us when we criticize others but won't deal with our own obvious "plank".

The first important factor regarding blind spots is to acknowledge that they exist. Without exceptional effort, we are truly blind to what is there. We need to ask the Lord to reveal to us our blind spots, those areas in our hearts and minds that we simply cannot see on our own. We need Him to give us the miracle of His clear sight.

Let's humbly come before His Throne of Grace and ask Him to reveal the blind spots in our hearts and minds, where we may be seeing ourselves as *wise in our own eyes*. Then let's ask Him to lead us in repentance and put us back on track, for His kingdom's use and His glory.

Today's Action: Let's read Proverbs 26 together, with a thirst for His truth and a willingness to yield our spirit to His control, His correction and His direction.

Do you see a person wise in their own eyes? There is more hope for a fool than for them.   Proverbs 26:12

Take Time to be Holy

Take time to be holy, speak oft with thy Lord;
Abide in Him always and feed on His Word.
Make friends of God's children,
        help those who are weak
Forgetting in nothing His blessing to seek.

Take time to be holy, the world rushes on;
Spend much time in secret with Jesus alone.
By looking to Jesus,
        like Him thou shalt be;
Thy friends in thy conduct His likeness shall see.

December 27   Expectations

And without faith it is impossible to please God, because anyone who comes to Him must believe that He exists and that He rewards those who earnestly seek Him.
                                                    Hebrews 11:6

We strive to believe with our whole heart that He is who He says He is; that He is God Almighty. And if we earnestly seek Him, then He will reward us, right? Yes, but...

Expectations. How they can trip us up in our walk. We can so easily start to define what our lives should look like as He "rewards" us for our faith and diligence. We begin to expect less stress, less pain, less illness, less heartbreak, more answers to our prayers, sometimes even miraculous answers. Surely our lives will just get rosier and rosier!

Ever so slowly, we begin to change our focus from Him and His plans and purposes, to ourselves and our comfort and pleasure. We begin to see any heartbreak in life as "undeserved"; any difficulty as "unnecessary". We can be caught off guard.

How can we keep our hearts full of faith when the unexpected shatters our world? Jesus tells us not to worry about our tomorrows (Matthew 6:34). All our tomorrows are under His control and His direction. In spite of any circumstance we encounter, we can choose to "Be still, and know that I am God" (Psalm 46:10). And Psalm 118:24 directs: "This is the day which the Lord hath made; we will rejoice and be glad in it" (KJV). What we can know for sure is that we have been given this moment, this day, to live. In childlike faith, we can choose to walk joyfully through this day, hand in hand with Him, and leave all our tomorrows in His loving and trustworthy care.

Let's come to Him with all the trust a child has in an all-wise Father. Let's rejoice today, giving Him all our expectations for tomorrow, confident that our prayers are being answered in His way, in His time, in His plan.

Today's Action: Let's read Proverbs 27, welcoming its reinforcement in wisdom for our lives.

Do not boast about tomorrow, for you do not know what a day may bring.
                                                    Proverbs 27:1

I Need Thee Every Hour

I need Thee ev'ry hour, most gracious Lord;
No tender voice like Thine can peace afford.
I need Thee, O I need Thee,
    ev'ry hour I need Thee!
O bless me now, my Savior - I come to Thee!

I need Thee ev'ry hour, stay Thou near by;
Temptations lose their pow'r when Thou art nigh.
I need Thee, O I need Thee,
    ev'ry hour I need Thee!
O bless me now, my Savior - I come to Thee!

December 28   Help My Unbelief

Does God heed our prayers if we have doubt? James says "But when you ask, you must believe and not doubt, because the one who doubts is like a wave of the sea, blown and tossed by the wind. That person should not expect to receive anything from the Lord." (James 1:6-7). It sure sounds like doubt would cause our prayers to go unheeded.

But does believing and not doubting mean having *no* doubt? Not likely. We probably will always have some lingering doubt. But we cannot ask in faith if we are *filled* with doubt.

In II Corinthians 5:7, we are told that we walk "by faith, not by sight". Walking by faith means we choose to believe, and then act on that belief in spite of our lingering doubt. We try to come to Him as unwavering as possible. And, just like a little child learning to walk, we can become more unwavering the more we practice "walking by faith".

Mark 9 details the event of the father who brought his demon-possessed child to Jesus. The father told Jesus "…if you can do anything, take pity on us and help us." He was not *filled* with faith. He didn't say to Jesus "I *know* you can do anything!" He was coming with what little faith he had, asking with an "if". Jesus responded "Everything is possible for him who believes." Mark reports that "Immediately the boy's father exclaimed, 'I do believe; help me overcome my unbelief!' " (Mark 9:24)

We can be so encouraged by this account. This father desired to believe with his whole heart. He had some faith, but he wasn't filled with faith. He knew he still had some unbelief. But he did not let his lingering doubt control him. He brought it to Jesus. That is a powerful example for us.

Let's come wholeheartedly with what little faith we have, asking Him to deal with our remaining doubt. Let us take Him at His word, rest in His promises, and ask for grace to trust Him more.

Today's Action: Let's read Proverbs 28 together, choosing to place our trust in Him alone.

Those who trust in the LORD will prosper; those who trust in themselves are fools.   Proverbs 28:25b, 26a

'Tis So Sweet to Trust in Jesus

'Tis so sweet to trust in Jesus,	Jesus, Jesus, how I trust Him!
Just to take Him at His word,	How I've proved Him o'er and o'er!
Just to rest upon His promise,	Jesus, Jesus, precious Jesus!
Just to know, "Thus saith the Lord."	O for grace to trust Him more!

December 29   Take Courage!

For the eyes of the LORD range throughout the earth to strengthen those whose hearts are fully committed to Him.   II Chronicles 16:9

Isn't that an amazing image to ponder? God Himself searches "to and fro throughout the whole earth to show Himself strong" (KJV) to those "whose hearts are fully committed to Him." He is looking for us; searching for us. Why? So He can help us; so He can deliver us. What an encouragement to stand firm in the faith. What a reason to take courage!

However, His deliverance is conditional. The verse before the verse quoted above says "when you relied on the LORD, He delivered" (II Chronicles 16:8). We have to choose to fully rely on Him. He alone has the ability to deliver. He alone is worthy of trust. He alone is worthy of praise.

Let's ask Him to again examine our hearts and commit to rely fully on Him, to put our trust in Him alone. Then we can take courage! He will deliver! The victory is His, and therefore ours through our Lord Jesus!

But for those of us who may still be pretending and have not fully turned from our wickedness, today's Proverbs chapter begins with yet another stern warning – *Whoever remains stiff-necked after many rebukes will suddenly be destroyed – without remedy* (Proverbs 29:1). Let's be careful that we are not stiff-necked, refusing to repent, or we will suddenly be destroyed - without remedy. How tragic!

Let's thank and praise Him for His incredible promise that He searches us out in order to show Himself strong to us, so that He can help us, so that He can deliver us. How amazing! Let's make sure our hearts are fully committed to Him and ask Him to fill us with courage for the battle ahead.

Today's Action: Let's read Proverbs 29 together, committed to heeding its warnings so we can avoid the way of the fool who is ensnared by sin; instead, we can walk as the righteous ones, redeemed by Jesus, and free to sing and be glad because of His great love for us.

Evildoers are snared by their own sin, but the righteous shout for joy and are glad.   Proverbs 29:6

Am I a Soldier of the Cross?

Am I a soldier of the cross?	Sure I must fight if I would reign -
A foll'wer of the Lamb?	Increase my courage, Lord!
And shall I fear to own His cause	I'll bear the toil, endure the pain,
Or blush to speak His name?	Supported by Thy Word.

December 30   Final Exam

Since we are surrounded by such a great cloud of witnesses, let us throw off everything that hinders and the sin which so easily entangles. And let us run with perseverance the race marked out for us.   Hebrews 12:1

This is our last opportunity to examine our hearts before going into battle. If you have not turned from that sin He has been rebuking you for, do it now! Before it's too late. Now. *Right now.*

We are not talking here about being sinless or perfect; none of us can be! But what we are dealing with is the attitude of our hearts. If we knowingly and rebelliously continue in sin, unwilling to fully repent and fully release it, then we would be well advised to lay down our weapons, step aside and not participate in this battle before us.

Let's face it. Your prayers will be hindered by your willful sin. Your sword won't be effective either if you are unwilling to allow your sword - His Word - to cut out that sin in your own life. You won't be able to expertly wield your weapons of warfare. You will be a laughing stock to our enemy. You risk being exposed for the hypocrite you are. You'd best excuse yourself before you are discovered and face expulsion.

Either choose a side, or step aside. We cannot fight with our whole heart if we have a divided heart. So let's get completely and fully right with God right now, or step aside.

Let's come before Almighty God, in humble submission to His kingship in our lives. Let's lay everything on the altar of sacrifice, and ask Him to reveal and strip away anything that may hinder our effectiveness in the battle ahead.

Today's Action: Let's read Proverbs 30 together. Let's allow ourselves to be filled with awe at the power of our Creator Commander, and submit ourselves to His fitting us for battle, even if that includes stripping away that easily ensnaring "secret" sin.

There are those who are pure in their own eyes and yet are not cleansed of their filth.   Proverbs 30:12

Is Your All on the Altar?

You have longed for sweet peace and for faith to increase,   Is your all on the altar of sacrifice laid?
And have earnestly, fervently prayed;   Your heart does the Spirit control?
But you cannot have rest or be perfectly blest   You can only be blest and have peace and sweet rest
Until all on the altar is laid.   As you yield Him your body and soul.

December 31   The Roar of the Father

*I looked for someone among them who would build up the wall
and stand before me in the gap on behalf of the land so I would not
have to destroy it, but I found no one.*   Ezekiel 22:30

The God of the universe is looking for intercessors to stand in the gap on
behalf of our land so He won't have to destroy it. He sees us. We have
answered the call and completed 30 days of preparation. But maybe we are
skeptical and think, "What difference can our prayers really make?"

Bible teacher Priscilla Shirer[xi] reminds us of a scene from *The Lion
King*.[xii] Little Simba is in trouble because he disobeyed his father's
command. His life is now threatened by the hyaenas. He tries his best to
roar, but all that comes out sounds more like a whimper. The hyaenas mock
him; "Is that the best you got?" As Simba tries again, from behind him
comes the roar of his father, Mufasa. Mufasa's powerful roar fills the cave
and echoes down the canyon walls, scattering the hyaenas in fear. That's the
roar of the father. That's the roar of our Father.

May that image fill our hearts with courage as we move forward
together and engage in this fight. We know, in answer to our desperate,
fervent, albeit whimpered cries, our Father, the Creator of heaven and
earth, the Lord of Hosts, God Almighty, will come with His roar to scatter
the enemy, and accomplish His will in the lives of His people and our land.

God promises "Call upon Me in the day of trouble; I will deliver you,
and you will honor Me" (Psalm 50:15). As His people, we are answering
His call to stand in the gap on behalf of our land and for those who either
cannot, or will not, speak for themselves.

Will our prayers be heard? Absolutely! Will we see the evidence? Not
necessarily. But since we walk by faith and not by sight (II Cor. 5:7), we
know the victory has already been won. He has called us to pray, and we
obey. Now, the battle belongs to the Lord. May we be His faithful warriors.

Today's Action: Let's read Proverbs 31 together and commit to
applying its instruction to our lives.

*Speak up for those who cannot speak for themselves, for the rights
of all who are destitute.*   Proverbs 31:8

To God Be the Glory

To God be the glory-great things He hath done	Praise the Lord, Praise the Lord, let the earth hear His voice!
So loved He the world that He gave us His Son,	Praise the Lord, Praise the Lord, let the people rejoice!
Who yielded His life an atonement for sin	O come to the Father thru Jesus the Son,
And opened the Lifegate that all may go in.	And give Him the glory - great things He hath done!

45

6

THE FINAL PREPARATION
FOR BATTLE

So He said to them, "This kind can come out by nothing but
prayer and fasting."   Mark 9:29 (NKJV)

A Time of Prayer and Fasting – New Year's Day

A call has gone out for a time of prayer and fasting on New Year's Day, January 1. Why has this call been issued? And what might this time look like in our individual lives?

Prayer is often accompanied by fasting in the Bible. As esteemed theologian, Wayne Grudem, writes, "Fasting expresses earnestness and urgency in our prayers; if we continued to fast, eventually we would die. Therefore, in a symbolic way, fasting says to God that we are prepared to lay down our lives that the situation be changed rather than that it continue."[xiii]

Fasting and prayer acknowledges that we are truly in dire straits. This is urgent business. The future of our nation may depend on it. The safety of our children may depend on it. The protection of religious liberty and our freedom to worship God may depend on it. The spread of Christianity around the world may depend on it. Who knows if we have not been called together to pray "for such a time as this" (Esther 4:14)?

Another reason to call for a time of fasting and prayer is that Jesus taught that some spiritual battles are so serious, they can only be dealt with through prayer and fasting (Matthew 17:21; Mark 9:29 NKJV). If we see this time as so pivotal in our nation's history, wouldn't it make sense to pull out all the stops, to do whatever we can to ensure the best possible outcome?

If we answer this call to pray and fast on New Year's Day, what would this look like in each of our individual life situations? That is a question that can only be answered by each of us individually seeking the Lord for ourselves. Some of us may be able to lead our entire family in a day of prayer and fasting, demonstrating how historical and critical this moment is. Some of us may be led to just take in liquid all day, fasting from solid food. Others may only be able to skip a meal or two because of the obligations we have. Yet others of us may have medical issues so we are not able to go without food, not even for a single meal. But everyone can give up something – second servings? dessert? Let's just not let this become legalistic. Let's each simply ask the Lord what He would have us do in obedience to this call to fast and pray.

More importantly than *what* we choose as a fast is *why* we choose to fast. If our motive is to be seen by others as more righteous, then our actions will not be blessed. Jesus instructs in Matthew 6:1 "Be careful not to practice your righteousness in front of others to be seen by them. If you do, you will have no reward from your Father in heaven." He then further instructs "When you fast, do not look somber as the hypocrites do, for they disfigure their faces to show others they are fasting. Truly I tell you, they have received their reward in full" (Matthew 6:16).

Jesus goes on to tell us the proper attitude in fasting: "But when you fast, put oil on your head and wash your face, so that it will not be obvious to others that you are fasting, but only to your Father, who is unseen; and your Father, who sees what is done in secret, will reward you" (Matthew 6:17-18).

Jesus did not say *"If* you fast..."* He said *"When* you fast..."* The assumption is that we will fast from time to time. But Jesus tells us to do it in such a way that it does not call attention to ourselves for the purpose of people's praise, but only to be seen by God Himself.

People judge by outward appearances; God looks at and judges our hearts (I Samuel 16:7). He is the only One whose praise we seek as we make a plan for New Year's Day. As He leads, we choose to set aside some portion or all of this day in fasting and prayer in advance of our momentous, coordinated attack on our enemy and his demonic forces.

Throughout this New Year's Day, as we focus our hearts and minds on the 50-day prayer challenge ahead, let's ask the Lord what He would like to accomplish through our prayers. What changes in the hearts and lives of us, His people, would be pleasing to Him? What areas of concern would He like us to bring to Him in prayer? And what would He like to see accomplished in the heart and life of our nation as a whole?

As we seek His face and listen to His direction, we may want to use the following space to record the concerns He brings to our mind. Then we can refer to this list during our 50 days of intercession and be reminded of His heart for us and our country.

Notes from Time of Prayer and Fasting:

_____

_____

_____

_____

_____

_____

_____

_____

_____

_____

_____

_____

7

SHOULDER TO SHOULDER

I looked for someone among them who would build up the wall and stand before me in the gap on behalf of the land so I would not have to destroy it, but I found no one.   Ezekiel 22:30

50 Days of Intercession

The final phase of this prayer project consists of 50 days of intercessory prayer. This part of the program begins January 2 and ends February 20. We come together as brothers and sisters in the Lord from all 50 States. Shoulder to shoulder, we stand in the gap on behalf of ourselves, our brothers and sisters in Christ, and our nation.

The book of Psalms will serve as our framework during these 50 days of prayer. Why Psalms? Psalms is a book of praise and petition to the Lord. The Psalms remind us to "Be still and know that I am God" (Psalm 46:10). They remind us that God alone is our refuge and strength (Psalm 46:1); He alone is our rock and salvation (Psalm 62:14); He alone is our shelter in times of trouble (Psalm 9:9). The Psalms also lead us in praise to Him for answering when we cry out to Him in repentance and dependence (Psalm 34:6).

The book of Psalms has been divided into 50 daily Psalm Reading (PR) assignments. Each State will be assigned a rotating 1/50th of the Psalms each day. Therefore, the entire book of Psalms will be lifted to the Lord for 50 days, with rotating sections being read by prayer warriors in each State.

Each State will begin with the Psalm Reading (PR) that matches that State's number when listed alphabetically among the 50 States. For example, Alabama is the first State when listed alphabetically. Therefore, on January 2nd, the first day of prayer, intercessors in Alabama will begin with Psalm Reading 1 (PR 1). But on that same day, Californians will begin with Psalm Reading 5 (PR 5) because California is the 5th of the 50 States alphabetically. Texans will begin with Psalm Reading 43 since Texas is the 43rd State in the alphabetical list of States. Each State then rotates daily through each of the 50 Psalm Readings.

An alphabetical listing of States, along with the first reading assignment, is provided on pages 54 and 55. Once you have determined what Psalm Reading (PR) division you will be starting with on our first day of prayer, you can simply fill in January 2 on the line next to your first assignment and then fill in the dates for the remaining 49 divisions through February 20.

For intercessors in the District of Columbia as well as various U. S. Territories, you can line up with any State that you prefer, or you can start by reading PR 1 with Alabama. However, since Wyoming is both the last and the least populated State, you may wish to join with them. Wyoming is the 50th State, so Wyoming intercessors will be starting with Psalm Reading 50 (PR 50) on January 2nd, moving to Psalm Reading 1 (PR 1) on January 3rd, continuing to rotate through to Psalm Reading 49 (PR 49) on the last day, February 20.

Each day of prayer will begin with our assigned Psalm reading for that day based on our State of residence, and each subsequent day will rotate through each of the 50 portions of Psalms. When read aloud, each Psalm reading will typically take an average of 5-7 minutes per day. This means that each of us as intercessors, spending around 5-7 minutes per day, will have read every word of the book of Psalms by the end of this 50-day period as we rotate progressively through each of the 50 Psalm readings.

As we read our respective Psalm reading selection for each day, let's ask the Lord to lead us in what He would like us to bring before Him in prayer that day. The subjects may change from day to day based on the Psalm reading selection for that day. Or some of us may have a particular burden on our hearts that will be the same throughout several or all of the 50 days. Let's simply ask Him to guide us in what He wants us to bring to Him in prayer.

The plan is simple:

1.   Find your State's ranking when listed alphabetically. The list is on pages 54-55.

2.   Start your first day of prayer, January 2, with the Psalm reading assignment that corresponds to your State's ranking.

3.   Proceed through the rest of the 50 Psalm readings chronologically each day until February 20.

4.   Daily devotions are provided that correspond with each of the Psalm reading divisions. They are intended to encourage and embolden us as we read Psalms to the Lord and then engage in intercession. Begin with the devotion that corresponds to your State's alphabetical position number, then continue to rotate daily through all 50 devotions and Psalm readings. Following this pattern, the entire book of Psalms will be read to the Lord each and every day for 50 days by prayer warriors from all 50 States.

We have submitted ourselves to Him during the 31 Days of Preparation so He can cleanse us and equip us to become powerful intercessors in this spiritual battle. Let's now engage the enemy and take back the territory that has been surrendered!

Let's lift up our praises and petitions to Him as intercessors from all 50 States, appealing to Him for repentance and revival of His people. Let's keep in mind that the purpose of these 50 days of dedicated prayer is to stand in the gap for our fellow Christians and for our nation as a whole. Let's ask the Lord to purify the hearts and lives of His people, returning us to our "first love" (Revelation 2:4). Let's pray that He will enable us, His people, to turn from our wicked ways, so that He, Almighty God, will forgive our sins and heal our land (II Chronicles 7:14).

Because of Jesus, our victory is assured! Our faithful fighting is all that remains to be done. As we cry out to Him over the next 50 days, He will hear our whole-hearted, desperate cries and empower them for the tearing down of strongholds, for the restoration of the hearts of His people and for the healing of our nation.

Let us together rejoice that He has called each one of us to the privilege of interceding at this time for His purposes to be accomplished in our lives and in the life of our nation. Let's prepare to engage, shoulder to shoulder, faithfully standing in the gap for our land!

May our nation be renewed as the beacon of hope and the bright light that it once was for His kingdom, and for the spreading of the gospel of good news to all the world.

Let the battle begin.

50 Psalm Reading Assignments

State	Date	Psalm Reading Divisions	
1. ALABAMA	5	**PR 1:** Psalms 1 – 5	❑
2. ALASKA	6	**PR 2:** Psalms 6 – 9	❑
3. ARIZONA	7	**PR 3:** Psalms 10 – 14	❑
4. ARKANSAS	8	**PR 4:** Psalms 15-17;19-20	❑
5. CALIFORNIA	9	**PR 5:** Psalm 18	❑
6. COLORADO	10	**PR 6:** Psalms 21 – 23	❑
7. CONNECTICUT	11	**PR 7:** Psalms 24 – 27	❑
8. DELAWARE	12	**PR 8:** Psalms 28 – 31	❑
9. FLORIDA	13	**PR 9:** Psalms 32 – 34	❑
10. GEORGIA	14	**PR 10:** Psalms 35, 38	❑
11. HAWAII	15	**PR 11:** Psalms 36 & 37	❑
12. IDAHO	16	**PR 12:** Psalms 39 – 42	❑
13. ILLINOIS	17	**PR 13:** Psalms 43 – 45	❑
14. INDIANA	18	**PR 14:** Psalms 46 – 49	❑
15. IOWA	19	**PR 15:** Psalms 50 – 52	❑
16. KANSAS	20	**PR 16:** Psalms 53 – 56	❑
17. KENTUCKY	2	**PR 17:** Psalms 57 – 59	❑
18. LOUISIANA	3	**PR 18:** Psalms 60 – 63	❑
19. MAINE	4	**PR 19:** Psalms 64 – 66	❑
20. MARYLAND	5	**PR 20:** Psalms 67 & 68	❑
21. MASSACHUSETTS	6	**PR 21:** Psalms 69 & 70	❑
22. MICHIGAN	7	**PR 22:** Psalms 71 & 72	❑
23. MINNESOTA	8	**PR 23:** Psalms 73 & 74	❑
24. MISSISSIPPI	9	**PR 24:** Psalms 75 – 77	❑

25. MISSOURI	_10_	**PR 25:** Psalm 78	❑
26. MONTANA	_11_	**PR 26:** Psalms 79 – 81	❑
27. NEBRASKA	_12_	**PR 27:** Psalms 82 – 85	❑
28. NEVADA	_13_	**PR 28:** Psalms 86 – 88	❑
29. NEW HAMPSHIRE	_14_	**PR 29:** Psalm 89	❑
30. NEW JERSEY	_15_	**PR 30:** Psalms 90 – 92	❑
31. NEW MEXICO	_16_	**PR 31:** Psalms 93 – 96	❑
32. NEW YORK	_17_	**PR 32:** Psalms 97 – 101	❑
33. NORTH CAROLINA	_18_	**PR 33:** Psalms 102 & 103	❑
34. NORTH DAKOTA	_19_	**PR 34:** Psalms 104, 108	❑
35. OHIO	_20_	**PR 35:** Psalm 105	❑
36. OKLAHOMA	_21_	**PR 36:** Psalm 106	❑
37. OREGON	_22_	**PR 37:** Psalms 107, 110	❑
38. PENNSYLVANIA	_23_	**PR 38:** Psalms 109, 111-112	❑
39. RHODE ISLAND	_24_	**PR 39:** Psalms 113 – ~~116~~ _115_	❑
40. SOUTH CAROLINA	_25_	**PR 40:** Psalms 117-118, ~~120~~ _116-_	❑
41. SOUTH DAKOTA	_26_	**PR 41:** Psalm 119:1-56	❑
42. TENNESSEE	_27_	**PR 42:** Psalm 119:57-112	❑
43. TEXAS	_28_	**PR 43:** Psalm 119:113-176	❑
44. UTAH	_29_	**PR 44:** Psalms ~~121~~ _120_ – 126	❑
45. VERMONT	_30_	**PR 45:** Psalms 127 – 132	❑
46. VIRGINIA	_31_	**PR 46:** Psalms 133-5;137,138	❑
47. WASHINGTON	_1_	**PR 47:** Psalms 136, 139	❑
48. WEST VIRGINIA	_2_	**PR 48:** Psalms 140 – 143	❑
49. WISCONSIN	_3_	**PR 49:** Psalms 144 – 146	❑
50. WYOMING	_4_	**PR 50:** Psalms 147 – 150	❑

I AM A DISCIPLE

The die has been cast.
I have stepped over the line.
The decision has been made.
I AM A DISCIPLE OF JESUS CHRIST.

I will not look back,
   let up,
   slow down,
   back away,
   or be still.

I no longer need preeminence,
   prosperity,
   position,
   promotions,
   praises,
   or popularity.

I do not have to be right,
   first,
   tops,
   recognized,
   regarded,
   or rewarded.

I now live by faith,
   love by patience,
   lift by prayer,
   and labor by power.

My pace is set.
My gait is fast.
My goal is Heaven.
My road is narrow.
My way is rough.
My companions few.
My Guide is reliable.
My mission is clear.

I cannot be bought,
   compromised,
   deterred,
   lured away,
   turned back,
   diluted,
   or delayed.

I will not flinch in the face of
sacrifice, hesitate in the presence
of adversity, negotiate at the table
of the enemy, pander at the pool
of popularity, nor meander in the
maze of mediocrity.

I will not give up,
   back up,
   let up,
   or shut up
   until I have prayed up,
   preached up,
   stored up and stayed up
   for the cause of Christ.
I AM A DISCIPLE OF JESUS CHRIST.

I must go 'til He returns,
   give until I drop,
   preach until all know,
   and work until He stops me.

And when He comes to get
His own, He will have no
trouble recognizing me.

My colors are flying high,
and they are clear for all to see.

I AM A DISCIPLE OF JESUS CHRIST.

Facing death, this was penned by an African minister martyred in the 1800's. Often called *I Am a Disciple*, it is also known as *The Creed of the Fellowship of the Unashamed*. "For I am not ashamed of the Gospel of Christ, for it is the power of God to salvation for everyone who believes." Romans 1:16

Reading 1: Psalms 1-5　　　　　　　　　　　Why?

The kings of the earth rise up and the rulers band together against the LORD and against His anointed, saying, "Let us break their chains and throw off their shackles."　　　　　　　　　　　　Psalm 2:2-3

When we look around, we often wonder "Why can't we just all get along?" Why is there such division, anger and hatred in families, communities, and nations? In particular, why is there persecution and martyrdom? Why will some people kill others simply because of their beliefs?

Psalm 2 explains it. Christians choose to live by God's moral standard as outlined in His Holy Word. We seek to please Him because He gave His life to redeem us. But unbelievers desire to please only themselves. They see God's moral standard as just spoiling their fun. So the goal of their rebellious, "enlightened" spirits is to break these "chains" and throw off these "shackles". This often includes punishing or eliminating those who stand up to their rebellion against God, who dare call their rebellion "sin".

Such was the case of the young minister martyred in Africa for his faith centuries ago. In reading his declaration on the opposite page, you can feel his determination, his will to stand firm in his faith. This infuriated his opponents all the more, to the point of killing him. But he knew that, no matter what they did, his past was redeemed; his future secure. He had nothing to fear, not even death.

As we intercede for each other and our nation, may we be encouraged by his words as they ring through the centuries. No matter what may come, may we boldly declare "I am a disciple of Jesus Christ." With Paul, may we firmly say, "I am not ashamed of the Gospel of Christ, for it is the power of God to salvation for everyone who believes" (Romans 1:16 NKJV).

And when He comes to claim His own, may He have no trouble recognizing us. May our colors fly high for all to see that we, too, are disciples of Jesus Christ.

O Jesus I Have Promised

O Jesus, I have promised to serve Thee to the end;
Be Thou forever near me, my Master and my Friend.
I shall not fear the battle if Thou art by my side,
Nor wander from the pathway if Thou wilt be my Guide.

Reading 2: Psalms 6-9   What is Man?

What is man that You are mindful of him?   Psalm 8:4

As a shepherd by trade, David likely spent many a dark night out with his sheep. One can imagine that he often "considered" the heavens, as he writes in Psalm 8. Observing the immensity of the universe, he marvels "What is man that You are mindful of him?" (Psalm 8:4)

If we contemplate the complexity of His creation, we too will marvel that He cares for each of us individually. If we try to wrap our minds around the fact that every hair on our head is numbered (Luke 12:7) and that He is "intimately acquainted" with all our ways (Psalm 139:3 AMP), it is too much for us to grasp.

Not only does He know all things about each of us, but He also cares about, and is involved in, the details of our lives. In Psalm 9, David reminds us that our God is a refuge for the oppressed, a defense in times of trouble, and that He will not forsake those who seek Him and place their trust in Him (Psalm 9:9-10). What comfort.

David also knew that sometimes we need times of trouble in order to recognize our need for the Lord. He petitions, "Put them in fear, O LORD, that the nations may know themselves to be but men" (Psalm 9:20 NKJV).

This is an appropriate prayer for us to pray today, not only over our nation and our world, but over each one of us individually. Only He can quicken our consciences, convicting of sin. Together, let's ask Him to put us all in an appropriate awe and fear of Him, so we see ourselves to be "but men".

May we all ask Him for His reality check, so we will see who we truly are - just sinful people in need of our Savior. Whether it is a need to repent and turn from sin, or a need for wisdom and provision to get through the next 24 hours, we all need Jesus.

This Is My Father's World (v. 3)

This is my Father's world - O let me ne'er forget
That tho the wrong seems oft so strong, God is the Ruler yet.
This is my Father's world! The battle is not done;
Jesus who died shall be satisfied, and earth and heav'n be one.

Reading 3: Psalms 10-14   Wise or a Fool?

The fool says in his heart, "There is no God." Psalm 14:1

Today's Psalms spend much time describing the fool. In arrogance and pride, the fool says "There is no God; He will never see" (Psalm 14:1; Psalm 10:11 NKJV). As a result, they boast of the cravings of their heart and boldly renounce God's principles; they celebrate wickedness, are corrupt, murder the innocent, and do "abominable works" (Psalms 10:3, 8, 11; 12:8; and 14:1 NKJV). Doesn't that describe much of our world today?

No one likes to be considered the fool. We tend to equate a fool with one who is ignorant and lacks intelligence. But taken in context, the Hebrew word translated here as "fool" refers to someone devoid of moral character, rather than someone lacking intelligence.

Many highly intelligent people deny the reality of God's existence. Why? It's not because they are ignorant. Instead, it's more likely an issue of pride. They think "No one's going to tell me what I can and can't do!" Tossing out God's moral compass, they choose to do whatever they please, whenever they please. They live for the moment, ignoring the reality of eternal consequences. Fools, indeed.

Jesus repeats this same thought in His parable of the wise and foolish builder. The wise man listened and built his life on the Word. When the storms of life hit, his house stood firm. However, the foolish man ignored the rock-solid foundation of God's ways, and built his house on sand instead. When faced with the realities of life, Jesus said "great was its fall" (Matthew 7:27 NKJV).

Let's ask the Lord today to show us if there are areas in our lives where we are not lining up with the building code of His Word. Let's be wise and anchor our lives on the solid rock of His truth. Let's intercede for those who have been blinded by the deceptions of the enemy. May they be given sight and see their need to build their lives in keeping with His ways.

We Have an Anchor

Will your anchor hold in the storms of life,
When the clouds unfold their wings of strife?
When the strong tides lift and the cables strain,
Will your anchor drift or firm remain?

We have an anchor that keeps the soul
Steadfast and sure while the billows roll,
Fastened to the Rock which cannot move,
Grounded firm and deep in the Savior's love.

Reading 4: Psalms 15-17; 19 & 20   Eternity

In Your presence is fullness of joy. Psalm 16:11 NKJV

In today's Psalms, David expresses grave concern for his life. But then he moves his focus from the difficulties of this temporal, earthly experience to the permanence of the eternal. "As for me", he says, "I shall be satisfied when I awake in Your likeness" (Psalm 17:15 NKJV).

When we turn our eyes from this world to the next, what a beautiful place to find rest for our souls. There are so many things beyond our control in this short experience we call life. Right now, it may seem like our difficulties will last forever. But this life will be over before we know it. Then we will experience fullness of joy in His presence forever.

Fullness of joy! We can't even begin to imagine what that would be like. In perfected bodies, we will have no more pain, no sickness, no sorrow; no more stresses, no anxiety, no uncertainty. It's hard to imagine what that will be like. But we know it will be more amazing than we can even begin to imagine. "Beloved, it has not yet been revealed what we shall be, but we know that when He is revealed, we shall be like Him, for we shall see Him as He is" (I John 3:2 NKJV).

May our hearts be filled with the wonder of it all - that He would love us so much that He would come and live a perfect life and die such a horrific death in order for us to be with Him for all eternity. Such love! Such joy! Such hope!

As we read these Psalms and intercede on behalf of each other and our nation, may we be energized with certainty today. Regardless of the circumstances we face today, they cannot impact our eternal destiny. In the twinkling of an eye, we will all be changed. So let's keep our eye on the eternal and, in what will seem like a blink, we will be with Him for all eternity.

O That Will Be Glory

When all my labors and trials are o'er	O that will be glory for me,
And I am safe on that beautiful shore,	Glory for me, glory for me;
Just to be near the dear Lord I adore	When by His grace I shall look on His face,
Will through the ages be glory for me.	That will be glory, be glory for me!

Reading 5: Psalms 18, ~~20~~   Fighting Fear

Some trust in chariots and some in horses, but
we trust in the name of the LORD our God.   Psalm 20:7

Psalm 18 is David's song of deliverance after God saved him from King Saul and his armies. David was being hunted by the King himself and his military forces. But David chose to trust in the Lord, and God rescued him in a mighty way.

David describes the awesome power God displayed in His rescue: The earth trembled, the mountains shook; He bowed the heavens and flew upon the wings of the wind; His voice thundered from the heavens; He sent out hailstones and fire; He sent His arrows and lightning, scattering and vanquishing the enemy (Psalm 18:7-14 NKJV).

Our mighty God rules the heavens and the earth. But David also knew He is attentive to the cries and heartaches of each one of His children. He knows our troubles, our burdens, and He knows our fears.

What is fear? It is a powerful tool of our enemy. What makes fear one of his most powerful tools? Because it is rooted in distrust. When there is uncertainty in our lives, it's hard to choose to simply trust God. We want to be in control; we want to fix it. Our focus is in an inappropriate place, because our eyes are locked in on ourselves and our circumstances. But there is no help to be found there. Our help only comes from the Lord, the maker of heaven and earth!

We join forces together in prayer today because we can trust our Almighty God to deliver us. We choose to trust Him in every circumstance and bring Him every fear. We choose to take "every thought into captivity to the obedience of Christ" (II Corinthians 10:5), by speaking truth to those fearful emotions our enemy tries to plant in our minds. Instead, we place our trust in the name of Him who alone is our strength, our rock, our fortress, our deliverer, our shield, our stronghold and our salvation.

Trusting Jesus

Simply trusting ev'ry day,
Trusting thru a stormy way;
Even when my faith is small,
Trusting Jesus - that is all.

Trusting as the moments fly,
Trusting as the days go by;
Trusting Him what e'er befall,
Trusting Jesus - that is all.

Reading 6: Psalms 21-23   Prophesy

All the ends of the world will remember and turn to the LORD...
Psalm 22:27a

Today's reading includes the familiar 23rd Psalm: "The LORD is my shepherd; I shall not want." What comfort is found in these words: "Yea, though I walk through the valley of the shadow of death, I will fear no evil, for You are with me" (Psalm 23:1, 4 NKJV).

Today's Psalms also include very specific details about Jesus' death, written nearly 1,000 years before they actually took place: "All those who see me ridicule me; they hurl insults; they shake their heads, saying, 'He trusted in the LORD; let Him rescue him.' A band of evil men has encircled me, they have pierced my hands and my feet; they divide my garments among them and cast lots for my clothing" (Psalm 22:7-8; 16; 18 NKJV).

After His resurrection, Jesus explained to His disciples why He had to die: " 'This is what I told you while I was still with you: everything must be fulfilled that is written about Me in the Law of Moses, the Prophets and the Psalms' " (Luke 24:44). How amazing that God Himself, in the person of Jesus Christ, validated the Old Testament in this way, including the Book of Psalms.

Toward the end of Psalm 22, there is prophesy that may be in the process of reaching fulfillment: "All the ends of the world will remember and turn to the LORD" (Psalm 22:27). Is it possible that part of the Lord's purpose in calling us to prayer at this time is to usher in the completion of this final prophecy?

May we be strengthened and emboldened as we read Psalms 21-23 to Him today and intercede for each other and our world. Let's pray that now would be the completion of the prophecy that "all the ends of the world will remember and turn to the Lord", including prodigals from every nation, tribe and tongue, because "dominion belongs to the LORD and He rules over the nations" (Psalm 22:28).

Jesus Shall Reign

Jesus shall reign where e'er the sun
Does his successive journeys run,
His kingdom spread from shore to shore
'Til moons shall wax and wane no more.

Reading 7: Psalms 24-27   A Greater Fear

The LORD is my light and my salvation - whom shall I fear?
Psalm 27:1a

Many Psalms were written when David was in real fear. His very life was threatened, first by King Saul and later even by his own son, Absalom. Fear can be a very real factor in all of our lives from time to time.

Fear can be a useful tool. It can help us realize our helplessness in and of ourselves. But also, a greater fear can cast out a lesser fear. By having a *greater fear* (respect or awe) for the God who preserves and protects, David could let go of his *lesser fear* of what man might do to him. Instead, he could choose to put his trust in God. David recognized that "The LORD is the stronghold of my life -" which allowed him to say, "of whom shall I be afraid" (Psalm 27:1b)?

A healthy fear of God's justice can also be very useful. Moses said "Do not be afraid; God has come to test you, so that the fear of God will be with you to keep you from sinning" (Exodus 20:20). An appropriate fear of God can also keep us from sinning.

As people, we always worship something – either God or ourselves. Our natural tendency is to please ourselves – always being concerned with self. Self *-ish*. We are called to be self - *less*; to die to self through the substitutionary death of Jesus, who died in our place.

As we read Psalms 24-27 to the Lord today, let us be comforted that "The earth is the Lord's and everything in it" (Psalm 24:1). He is, and always will be, on His Throne. Nothing that happens is a surprise to Him. As we come before Him in prayer, let's ask Him to use our fears to bring all of us to the end of ourselves, to turn us away from our sin, and draw us back to Himself. Then we can face all of our futures without any fear.

He Hideth My Soul

A wonderful Savior is Jesus my Lord,
A wonderful Savior to me;
He hideth my soul in the cleft of the rock,
Where rivers of pleasure I see.

He hideth my soul in the cleft of the rock
That shadows a dry, thirsty land;
He hideth my life in the depths of His love,
And covers me there with His hand,
    and covers me there with His hand.

Reading 8: Psalms 28-31 — In His Hands

You are my God. My times are in Your hands. Psalm 31:14b-15a

In these psalms, David not only powerfully reminds us of who our God is, but also why He alone can be trusted with the concerns of our lives: God alone "sits enthroned above the flood; The LORD is enthroned as King forever" (Psalm 29:10).

David leads us by example in choosing to trust, in choosing to put his hope in God alone. David tells us "But I will trust in You, O LORD; I say 'You are my God.' My times are in Your hands" (Psalm 31:14-15). What a place of peace and refuge, a place of trust and rest. Regardless of how uncertain or difficult our circumstances are or may become, we can choose to trust Him as we remind ourselves of this truth: Our times are in His hands.

David ends today's reading with this encouragement: "Be strong and take heart, all you who hope in the LORD" (Psalm 31:24). So let us choose to put our hope in the LORD. Then we can be of good courage, because He promises to strengthen our hearts.

The best way to allow Him to strengthen our hearts is to immerse ourselves in His Word. The truth that He works all things together for the good of those who love Him (Romans 8:28) is a wonderful truth to encourage our trust. The fact that He has gone to prepare a place for us (John 14:2) is another reason for hope. The promise that nothing can separate us from His love (Romans 8:38-39) and that He is with us even to the end of the world (Matthew 28:20) are even more reasons to have hope and not be afraid.

As we read these Psalms to Him, let's remember these truths: He is sovereign. He is enthroned as King forever. And He is working out His will, in His way, and in His time. May He direct us and fill us with courage as we engage in battle today.

Moment by Moment

Dying with Jesus by death reckoned mine,
Living with Jesus a new life divine,
Looking to Jesus 'til glory doth shine -
Moment by moment, O Lord, I am Thine.

Moment by moment I'm kept in His love,
Moment by moment I've life from above;
Looking to Jesus 'til glory doth shine,
Moment by moment, O Lord, I am Thine.

Reading 9: Psalms 32-34   Firm Forever

The LORD foils the plans of the nations;
But the plans of the LORD stand firm forever.   Psalm 33:10a; 11a

As we look around us, it is easy to become disheartened and discouraged. Our world, in many ways, feels like it is spinning out of control, and it doesn't look to us like there is any easy way back.

That's when it is comforting to remind ourselves of the truth. Our God Almighty, Maker of heaven and earth, is still – and forever will be – firmly in control. He is the One who simply spoke and the heavens came into being. He created all "their starry host by the breath of His mouth" (Psalm 33:6). Let's dwell on that one truth for a moment.

According to statistics from worldometer.com, the current world population is around 8 billion people. Scientific documents from physicsoftheuniverse.com report there are approximately 100 billion galaxies in just the observable universe, with an estimated minimum of 10 billion trillion stars. Some estimate there may be up to 200 billion trillion stars! But if we take just 10 billion trillion stars and divide them among all 8 billion people on the planet, everyone would have over a trillion stars! And each was created by "the breath of His mouth". Imagine blowing your breath over your hand and 10 billion trillion stars are scattered throughout 100 billion galaxies! Absolutely incomprehensible, yet absolutely true.

The Gospel of John reveals this truth about Jesus: "In the beginning was the Word, and the Word was with God, and the Word was God. He was in the beginning with God. All things were made through Him, and without Him nothing was made that was made" (John 1:1-3 NKJV). Also absolutely incomprehensible, yet absolutely true.

As we read today's Psalms to Him, let's rejoice that there is nothing and no one who is able to alter His plans and His purposes. Let's remind ourselves as we fervently pray that there is *absolutely nothing* too difficult for Him. The plans of Almighty God stand firm forever. Period.

The Solid Rock

My hope is built on nothing less   On Christ, the solid Rock, I stand -
Than Jesus' blood and righteousness;   All other ground is sinking sand,
I dare not trust the sweetest frame,   All other ground is sinking sand.
But wholly lean on Jesus' name.

Reading 10: Psalms 35, 38   He Will Hear

For in You, O LORD, I hope; You will hear, O LORD my God.
Psalm 38:15 NKJV

In these two Psalms, David complains about the painful circumstances in his life, some due to the actions of others and some due to his own sin. In both Psalms, however, we find David leading us back from a focus on himself to a focus on our God.

In Psalm 35, David is extremely upset about other people wanting to harm him. He pleads with God to bring pain, destruction and judgment on his enemies. After 27 verses of complaining about his enemies, he changes his focus and says "My tongue will speak of Your righteousness and of Your praises all day long" (Psalm 35:28 NKJV).

In Psalm 38, David details the pain he is suffering as a result of his own actions, which he labels as "my sinful folly" (Psalm 38:5). Instead of pain from other people, he is experiencing the judgment of God because of his sin: "Your arrows pierce me deeply, and your hand presses me down. There is no soundness in my flesh because of Your anger, nor any health in my bones because of my sin" (Psalm 38:2-4 NKJV). But once again, David brings his focus back to the Lord. "For in You, O LORD, I hope; You will hear, O LORD my God" (Psalm 38:15 NKJV).

As we turn our focus to Him today in reading His Word and intercession, let's remember that in spite of any circumstance, we will find peace when we turn our focus back to our Almighty God. No matter what we face today, whether a result of the actions of others, or our own foolishness and sin, the remedy cannot be found in ourselves. It can only be found in the Lord. Only He can right the wrongs; only He can bring forgiveness and healing; only He can restore the joy of our salvation. Because we know He hears and answers, let's take our burden to the Lord and leave it there.

Leave It There

If the world from you withhold of its silver and its gold,
And you have to get along with meager fare,
Just remember, in His Word,
   how He feeds the little bird -
Take your burden to the Lord and leave it there.

Leave it there, leave it there,
Take your burden to the Lord and leave it there;
If you trust and never doubt,
   He will surely bring you out -
Take your burden to the Lord and leave it there.

Reading 11: Psalms 36, 37   Rest in the Waiting

Rest in the LORD, and wait patiently for Him. Psalm 37:7a NKJV

Sometimes we can read something without it really registering in our hearts and minds. "Rest in the Lord, and wait patiently for Him" can be one of those phrases. We can glance at it and say, "Yes, I agree." But what does it look like to rest in Him and wait patiently?

There is much going on in the world around us that can cause us to be restless. Things are uncertain; people are unreliable; we feel vulnerable, unprotected. We don't know what the future holds and we don't like that feeling of not being in control. But the truth is that even when things *felt* certain, when we felt we could rely on people and we felt protected and secure, we weren't any more in control than we are right now. We just *felt* like we had control. People have had their lives turned up-side-down in the blink of an eye since time began.

David tells us that fretting or worrying about it only causes us harm (Psalm 37:8). Instead, he tells us to rest in the Lord and wait patiently for Him. What David is saying is to get our eyes off our circumstances (which are *always* beyond our control), and lift our focus to the Lord (who is *always* in control).

David goes on to tell us how to keep that perspective: he says to wait *patiently.* He knows better than to just tell us to wait. How impatient we can be in the waiting! And how disturbing that impatience is to our peace.

So, as we read these Psalms to the Lord today and fervently intercede, let's choose to rest in Him, our sovereign God. Let's determine to wait *patiently* for Him, casting *all* our care on Him, because He cares for us (I Peter 5:7). And let's choose to rest in the protection He offers to our hearts and minds as we take refuge under the shadow of His wings (Psalm 36:7).

Under His Wings

Under His wings I am safely abiding,
Tho the night deepens and tempests are wild;
Still I can trust Him - I know He will keep me,
He has redeemed me and I am His child.

Under His wings, under His wings,
Who from His love can sever?
Under His wings, my soul shall abide,
Safely abide forever.

Reading 12: Psalms 39-41 Just A Vapor

Certainly every man at his best state is but vapor. Psalm 39:5c NKJV

We don't like to think of our lives as just a vapor. But what exactly is a vapor? It is here one moment, and gone the next. But like a spray of cologne, it can be pleasingly powerful in the moment. It is not simply *nothing*; it's just not long-lasting. That may be a profitable perspective regarding our lives.

Our days are limited, passing quickly, here today and gone tomorrow. But the Lord has purpose in the precise number of days He has allotted each of us. He instructs us to "redeem the time" (Ephesians 5:16 NKJV), but how do we do that?

First, we can be encouraged that Jesus' time of public ministry was only three years, so whatever time we have left can still be used to impact His kingdom. It's not the amount of time that is important. It's how we allow Him to direct our time.

Secondly, we can diligently study and implement His Word; then seek to hear His voice and follow His direction. In the midst of trials, there are people who need to hear His gospel of love and forgiveness. We may be an encouragement to others as they watch us endure and remain faithful. For others, we may be the only "Bible" they ever read as we walk in love and forgiveness made possible only through the Holy Spirit living in us. We can determine to use the remaining days of our lives to bring glory to Him.

As we deal with this temporary life and the ravages of sin in this world, let's remember this is not our home. We are just passing through. In a moment, in the twinkling of an eye, every pain will be gone, every sorrow forgot, and we will spend a joyous eternity with each other and with our Redeeming Lord. May that truth energize us today as we fervently intercede on behalf of our loved ones, our nation and our world.

When We All Get to Heaven

Sing the wondrous love of Jesus,	When we all get to heaven,
Sing His mercy and His grace;	What a day of rejoicing that will be!
In the mansions bright and blessed	When we all see Jesus,
He'll prepare for us a place.	We'll sing and shout the victory.

Reading 13: Psalms 42-45   Like a Yo-Yo

Why are you cast down, O my soul? Hope in God..."
Psalm 42:5a, c NKJV

The theme of "Why are you down? Look up!" is repeated at least three times in our Psalm reading today, so let's spend a little time with it.

We all know that it is a "downer" when we focus on our world and our circumstances. This life can never be paradise because of sin.

We also know that we should "look up", knowing that this life is as temporary as a vapor, that we are aliens in this world, and that we are just passing through on our way to our permanent home in heaven, where Jesus is preparing a place for us (John 14:2).

But if we know all of these truths, why do we often struggle with the constant "yo-yo" of having to turn our "downs" into "ups"?

If we could just make it a "one and done" proposition, never to struggle again, we would feel so good, so proud of ourselves, and think "I've got this." Instead, the continuing "down and up" is a helpful reminder that we always need the Lord, so let's embrace it.

Our Psalms today also remind us that help does not come from ourselves. We cannot save ourselves. It is only God's arm, God's strength, God's power (Psalm 44:3). So our fervent intercession is exactly what we are supposed to do in order to bring His change in this world for His kingdom purposes. It's all by God, not us. But He gives us the privilege of participating in bringing about His kingdom through prayer.

The remedy repeated throughout our Psalms today is: "Hope in God, for I shall *yet* praise Him" (Psalm 42:5 – emphasis added NKJV). What a helpful and hopeful instruction to our souls. It speaks of a time that we can *know* is coming, a time of deliverance and rejoicing. It is future-focused, acknowledging that our all-powerful, all-wise God is working out *all* things in His way, in His time and for His glory.

Praise Him! Praise Him!

Praise Him! Praise Him!
Jesus, our blessed Redeemer,
Sing, O earth-His wonderful love proclaim!
Hail Him! Hail Him!
Highest archangels in glory,
Strength and honor give to His holy name.

Like a shepherd Jesus will guard His children -
In His arms He carries them all day long:
Praise Him! Praise Him!
Tell of His excellent greatness,
Praise Him! Praise Him!
Ever in joyful song!

Reading 14: Psalms 46-49   Even Then...

Therefore we will not fear, though the earth give way... Psalm 46:2

Today's psalm reading begins with these powerful words: "God is our refuge and strength, an ever-present help in trouble. Therefore we will not fear, though the earth give way and the mountains fall into the heart of the sea; though its waters roar and foam and the mountains quake with their surging" (Psalm 46:1-3). That's a pretty dramatic turning up-side-down of our world.

Sometimes it feels as though our world is crashing in around us. For some of us, it may literally be, as we suffer persecution or famine, with death and destruction on every side. But God says, *even then*, we can choose not to be afraid. Why? Because He sits on His holy Throne as He rules the nations (Psalm 47:8).

After describing this chaotic scenario, God says He will help "just at the break of dawn" (Psalm 46:5 NKJV). What is "the break of dawn"? It marks the end of night. When our lives feel like we are in the darkest of nights, take courage; He promises He is coming "just at the break of dawn."

Psalm 46 continues with words describing our world today: "Nations are in uproar, kingdoms fall;" but then comforts with these words: "Come and see the works of the LORD, the desolations He has brought on the earth. He makes wars cease to the ends of the earth; He breaks the bow and shatters the spear; He burns the chariots with fire" (Psalm 46:6-9). Talk about our God taking an active role in the affairs of men!

Surprisingly, the very next verse is God's directive to be still: "Be still, and *know* that I am God" (Psalm 46:10 – emphasis added). As we come in intercession, let's quiet our minds in the midst of our circumstances and speak truth to our hearts. Through all the storms of this temporary life, He has promised He will be with us *always*, "even to the end of the age" (Matthew 28:20).

Rock of Ages

Rock of Ages, cleft for me,	While I draw this fleeting breath,
Let me hide myself in Thee;	When my eyes shall close in death,
Let the water and the blood,	When I rise to worlds unknown
From Thy wounded side which flowed,	And behold Thee on Thy throne,
Be of sin the double cure,	Rock of Ages, cleft for me,
Save from wrath and make me pure.	Let me hide myself in Thee.

Create in me a clean heart, O God, and
renew a steadfast spirit within me.   Psalm 51:10

Psalm 51 was written after the prophet Nathan confronted David about his adultery with Bathsheba. Not only did David commit adultery, but then he committed murder to cover up his adultery. How could God forgive someone guilty of such grievous sins?

Decades before, God had rejected Saul as king. Why? Because Saul had not waited for Samuel before Saul made a sacrifice to the Lord. It seems like such a small thing to us, but it caused God to take away Saul's kingdom and give it to "a man after His own heart" – the humble shepherd David (I Samuel 13:14).

Did God not know that David would commit adultery, as well as a cover-up murder, during his reign as king? Of course, He did. So why did God reject Saul for such a little thing, but forgive David for such grave sins? That doesn't make sense to us. Why? Because we like to rank sins, judging some sins as worse than others.

Thankfully, God doesn't judge us by our sins. God says "man looks at the outward appearance" but He "looks at the heart" (I Samuel 16:7). The difference between Saul and David was the condition of their heart. After acknowledging his sin, David had "a broken and a contrite heart" (Psalm 51:17).

We can rejoice that, no matter how grievous, *no* sin is unforgiveable - if we come to Him in repentance. Then He lovingly says our sins are forgiven; so "go and sin no more" (John 8:11 NKJV). Then He can restore to us a spirit that is determined to be steadfast in living a life pleasing to Him (Psalm 51:10).

May these truths encourage us as we read these Psalms and fervently intercede on behalf of all those blinded by the deceptions of the enemy. May the Lord break our hearts for the lost and "give His light to those who sit in darkness and the shadow of death" (Luke 1:79 NKJV).

Grace Greater Than Our Sin

Marvelous grace of our loving Lord,	Grace, grace, God's grace,
Grace that exceeds our sin and our guilt!	Grace that will pardon and cleanse within;
Yonder on Calvary's mount outpoured -	Grace, grace, God's grace,
There where the blood of the lamb was spilt.	Grace that is greater than all our sin!

Reading 16: Psalms 53-56   Tears in a Bottle

You number my wanderings; put my tears into Your bottle;
*   are they not in Your book?*   Psalm 56:8 NKJV

A study of David's life reveals he had many times of great sorrow, including deep remorse for his sins of adultery and murder, painful wounds from the betrayal of friends, and intense grief with the death of two sons. He also had many times when he was fleeing for his life.

In the midst of these dark times, David reminds himself that God is not only powerful, but deeply personal. He sees; He keeps a record of our troubles and our tears.

When writing these psalms, David was hiding from King Saul (Psalm 54), was betrayed by friends (Psalm 55), and was a Philistine prisoner (Psalm 56). He had good reason to be fearful and downcast. He was not experiencing God's deliverance in, nor from, these moments. But he writes "Whenever I am afraid, I will trust in You." and twice he repeats: "In God I have put my trust; I will not fear. What can mere man do to me?" (Psalm 56:3-4, 11 NKJV)

If we are walking in fear today, let's follow David's example in Psalm 56:3: "Whenever I am afraid, I will trust in You." If we are carrying a burden today, David says "Cast your burden on the LORD and He shall sustain you" (Psalm 55:22 NKJV). And we can choose to rejoice with David, "For You have delivered me from death and my feet from stumbling, that I may walk before God in the light of life" (Psalm 56:13).

Our God knows all the details of our lives, from beginning to end. Nothing is a surprise to Him. He not only knows the number of our days before we were born (Psalm 139:16), but He knows the number of hairs on our head (Luke 12:7). When we truly grasp how intimately He knows us and how deeply He loves us, we can more fully and completely trust Him with every detail of our lives.

Day by Day

Day by day and with each passing moment,
Strength I find to meet my trials here;
Trusting in my Father's wise bestowment,
I've no cause for worry or for fear.

He whose heart is kind beyond all measure,
Gives unto each day what He deems best -
Lovingly, its part of pain and pleasure,
Mingling toil with peace and rest.

Reading 17: Psalms 57-59   It's All About Him

Be exalted, O God, above the heavens;
let Your glory be above all the earth.   Psalm 57:5 NKJV

Psalms 57-59 were written by David when he was in extreme circumstances. He was in constant fear for his life because King Saul and his men were hunting him down to kill him. Can we even begin to imagine the fear, frustration and anger that David felt?

The young shepherd boy had become a hero in Israel because he had defeated the giant Goliath. But instead of being honored, he was hiding in caves, hunted down, running for his life. Why? All because of jealousy and envy. Saul could not stand David's popularity, so he ordered his death. At times, Saul even accompanied his men in search of David.

David had every reason to be frustrated with God's timing and angry with God. It appeared as if God was not doing anything to right the wrongs and rescue him. But that did not deter David's trust in the Lord. In the midst of his difficulties, David says "My soul trusts in You; and in the shadow of Your wings I will make my refuge, until these calamities have passed by" (Psalm 57:1 NKJV).

David did not deny his difficulties. But David understood that God's purposes outweigh any temporary trials we face. After listing his troubles, he immediately shifts his focus to the eternal purposes of God: "Be exalted, O God, above the heavens; let Your glory be above all the earth." David is essentially saying "It's not about me; it's all about You."

This is the same mindset we find in Jesus prior to His crucifixion. After asking if the cup of suffering can pass, Jesus concludes with "Nevertheless, not My will, but Yours, be done" (Luke 22:42-43 NKJV).

Let's ask the Lord today to help us move our focus from our temporary trials to His eternal purposes, remembering that the purpose of our life is all about Him, being useful vessels for His kingdom and bringing glory to Him alone.

I Am Thine, O Lord

I am Thine, O Lord - I have heard Thy voice,
And it told Thy love to me;
But I long to rise in the arms of faith
And be closer drawn to Thee.

Draw me nearer, nearer, nearer, blessed Lord,
To the cross where Thou hast died;
Draw me nearer, nearer, nearer, blessed Lord,
To Thy precious, bleeding side.

Reading 18: Psalms 60-63   Fill and Spill

When my heart is overwhelmed,
lead me to the rock that is higher than I.   Psalm 61:2 NKJV

When we hear the term "overwhelmed", we can easily identify with it, can't we? In our busy world, it is easy to feel overwhelmed with all the things we have to do. But this verse is talking about an overwhelming of our hearts.

Our hearts can feel overwhelmed with anxiety, pain and disappointment. It is during these times of fear, uncertainty and heartache that David encourages us to ask the Lord to lead us to the rock that is higher than our circumstances. That rock, that stability, that firm foundation is found in Him alone.

David further instructs us to "Trust in Him at all times, you people; Pour out your heart before Him. God is a refuge for us" (Psalm 62:8 NKJV). David doesn't just say trust God some of the time; David says *all* of the time. He encourages us to pour out our hearts before Him because He is a refuge for us.

What happens when we pour out our hearts to Him? We empty our hearts of our fears, our hurts, and our vain imaginings. An empty heart is a heart that He can then fill with His love, His peace and His comfort. Wouldn't we rather walk around with hearts filled with His love, peace and comfort instead of our own fear, worries and pain?

The beauty of having our hearts filled by Him is that these blessings can then spill over into the hearts of those He brings across our path. We can be used by Him to pour His love, His peace, and His comfort into the lives of others. *Fill and spill.*

As we all open our hearts to His love, peace and comfort, we will discover with David that "Your unfailing love is better than life itself" (Psalm 63:3 NLT). Why? Because, in His lovingkindness, He died to purchase our salvation, so we can live together with Him for all eternity (I Thessalonians 5:10).

A Shelter in the Time of Storm

The Lord's our Rock, in Him we hide -	O Jesus is a Rock in a weary land,
A shelter in the time of storm;	A weary land, a weary land;
Secure whatever ill betide -	O Jesus is a Rock in a weary land,
A shelter in the time of storm.	A shelter in the time of storm.

Reading 19: Psalms 64-66　　　How Mighty is Our God

By awesome deeds in righteousness You will answer us,
O God of our salvation.　　　　　　　Psalm 65:5a NKJV

When we think of God, what do we imagine? Do we think of someone like a president or dictator, who orders people around and tells them what to do? Or do we think of an angry old man, wagging his finger at all the sinners in the world, just waiting to rain down fire and brimstone in judgment? Or maybe we imagine an inexplicable force of some type that miraculously set the universe in order, someone who just "wound up the clock" but then walked away?

None of those images fit the God of the Bible. In just our Psalms for today, David describes God as the One "who established the mountains by His strength, being clothed with power;" He stills "the noise of the seas, the noise of their waves, and the tumult of the peoples." David declares, "How awesome are Your works! Through the greatness of Your power, Your enemies shall submit themselves to You. All the earth shall worship You." David then invites us to "Come and see the works of God: He is awesome in His doing toward the sons of men. His eyes observe the nations; He rules by His power forever" (Psalm 65:6-7; Psalm 66:3-7 NKJV).

This is the God of the Bible. This is the powerful God we serve. This is the One who rebukes the winds and the waves. In gently chiding His disciples for their fear during the storm on the Sea of Galilee, Jesus said "Why are you fearful, O you of little faith?" (Matthew 8:26 NKJV) It was because they didn't really understand that He was God. They said "Who can this be, that even the winds and the sea obey Him?"

Let's remind ourselves today of how truly powerful our God is. As Creator, He simply spoke the entire universe into being. There is *nothing* too difficult for Him. In awesome deeds, He *will* answer us because He is the God of our salvation.

A Mighty Fortress

A mighty fortress is our God,	For still our ancient foe,
A bulwark never failing;	Doth seek to work us woe -
Our helper He amid the flood,	His craft and pow'r are great,
Of mortal ills prevailing.	And armed with cruel hate,
	On earth is not his equal.

Reading 20: Psalms 67, 68   The Chariots of God

The chariots of God are twenty thousand,
*   even thousands of thousands;*   Psalm 68:17 NKJV

Our inclination is to think of God as just an observer of the affairs of men. We may feel it is all up to us to "straighten out this mess" in our world today. But David reminds us of the truth. Our God is in charge, and He can be trusted to provide for those looking to Him.

Our Almighty God "rides on the clouds, on the heaven of heavens"; He gives the word and "kings of armies flee"; He scatters "the peoples who delight in war". David puts the exclamation point on this topic by saying "The chariots of God are twenty thousand, even thousands of thousands" (Psalm 68:4, 11-12, 17, 30, 33 NKJV).

This verse reminds us of Elisha and his fearful servant when surrounded by a massive Syrian army. Elisha tells his servant "Do not fear, for those who are with us are more than those who are with them." Then Elisha asks God to open the servant's eyes so he can see the army of God: "The mountain was full of horses and chariots of fire all around Elisha." God protected them far better than man ever could (II Kings 6:16-17 NKJV).

Accounts of God's miraculous intervention are not limited to the Bible. One of the more recent examples is the testimony of Air Force Capt. Scott O'Grady, who was shot down over Bosnia in 1995. Enemy soldiers walked right by him while searching in broad daylight and did not see him. He gives God all the glory for supernaturally protecting him.[xiv]

Let's remind ourselves again of the truth: our God remains firmly in control, even when it may not look that way to our earthly eyes. Nothing and no one can thwart His plans. Not even a sparrow falls without His knowledge (Matthew 10:29), so we need not fear. No matter what our circumstances may be, our Heavenly Father will care for us.

God Will Take Care of You

Be not dismayed whate'er betide,   God will take care of you,
God will take care of you;   Thru every day, o'er all the way;
Beneath His wings of love abide,   He will take care of you,
God will take care of you.   God will take care of you.

Reading 21: Psalms 69, 70   His Reputation

Let not those who seek You be confounded because of me...
Psalm 69:6b

David spends most of today's Psalm reading bemoaning his circumstances. He complains to God about the unfairness of life, and asks God come to his aid and bring destruction and judgment on his enemies. He is totally focused on His circumstances and crying out to God for relief.

But suddenly, in the midst of his bewailing, he asks the Lord "Let not those who seek You be confounded because of me" (Psalm 69:6b). He moves from being consumed about his own reputation to being concerned about how his behavior might be affecting God's reputation. He willingly admits that He is not perfect, writing "O God, You know my foolishness; and my sins are not hidden from You" (Psalms 69:5).

Are we equally concerned about how our behavior affects God's reputation? The most common criticism the world has about Christians is that they see us as hypocrites. They say our walks don't match our talk.

When people watch us in action, would they say we are more loving, more honest, more generous, and more forgiving than the rest of the world? Are we less selfish, less prideful, less gossipy, and less self-righteous than our non-Christian friends?

Let's take the world's criticism to the Lord and ask if there is anything that we think, say or do that does not reflect well on Him. As redeemed children of God, we desire to represent Him well. We want people to come to a saving knowledge of the truth (I Timothy 2:4). We don't want to be a stumbling block for people seeking Christ. But we are not perfect, and none of us ever will be, this side of heaven.

Let's come before our Refiner, and ask Him to reveal any dross that is marring a clear reflection of Him. Then let's confess, repent and rejoice that "He is faithful and just to forgive us our sins and to cleanse us from all unrighteousness" (I John 1:9 NKJV).

Jesus Paid It All

I hear the Savior say,
"Thy strength indeed is small!
Child of weakness, watch and pray,
Find in Me thine all in all."

Jesus paid it all,
All to Him I owe;
Sin had left a crimson stain -
He washed it white as snow.

Reading 22: Psalms 71, 72   Precious

...and precious shall be their blood in His sight. Psalm 72:14b

We know that our God is so intimately acquainted with all of our ways that He knows every hair on our head, He knows the number of our days, He even knows our thoughts and the words we are about to say before we even say them (Psalm 139:4). So it shouldn't surprise us that our blood - which could be interpreted to represent our life and/or our death - is "precious in His sight."

That is a nearly unfathomable thought, isn't it? The God who spoke all the universe into being and holds all things together by the power of His word (Hebrews 1:3), is so personal that all the moments of each one of our lives, even our very blood, is *precious* to Him.

Oh, that we could truly grasp how wide and how long and how high and how deep is the love of God for each one of us (Ephesians 3:18). What a difference that would make as we face each fear, each trial, and each loss in this fleeting experience of life. It would make it so much easier to run to Him with every fear or anxious thought, to simply trust Him through every trial, and to be comforted by Him in every sadness and loss.

Let us remind ourselves that our old life has been crucified with Christ, and the new life we now live is Christ living in us (Galatians 2:20). Therefore, our life, which is now actually His life living in and through us, would, of course, be precious to Him. What an astounding truth!

As we read Psalms 71 and 72 to the Lord today, and stand in the gap in intercession, let's re-commit to using our lives to bring glory to Him in all we do (I Corinthians 10:31). And no matter what circumstance we face, let us continue to place our trust and hope in Him alone, because He alone is our rock, our refuge and our fortress (Psalm 71:1-3).

O the Deep, Deep Love of Jesus

O the deep, deep love of Jesus -
Vast, unmeasured, boundless, free!
Rolling as a mighty ocean
In its fullness over me;

Underneath me, all around me,
Is the current of Thy love -
Leading onward, leading homeward,
To my glorious rest above.

Reading 23: Psalms 73, 74   Hand In Hand

You hold me by my right hand. Psalm 73:23b

Sometimes as adults, we feel responsible for everything. It feels appropriate to worry, to try to control everything. But Jesus says that we need to become like little children if we want to see the kingdom of heaven (Matthew 18:3). He didn't mean we should become childish, acting immaturely or irresponsibly. He meant we should become *childlike* in trusting our Heavenly Father.

Let's take a moment to think back on our days as a child. Can we remember a time just walking hand in hand with a parent or trusted adult? Let's pull up that moment, complete with all its emotion, and dwell on it for a bit.

We probably skipped along, joyful and content to be wherever we were at that moment. We didn't have a care in the world. We weren't worried about tomorrow; we didn't carry any guilt about yesterday's mistakes. We felt we could trust that we would be protected and provided for, and that was all it took to be content.

That's exactly the image described in Psalm 73. The writer rejoices that the Lord is near him at *all* times, holding him by the hand. Therefore, he knows the Lord will "guide me with Your counsel, and afterward receive me to glory" (Psalm 73:24).

What a marvelous visual of the truth! As we walk hand in hand with Him, He will lead us through each day until He take us to glory. We just need to remind ourselves to stay in communion with Him, our Vine, and turn to Him in childlike trust any time we are afraid.

As we intercede today, Let's welcome His presence, allowing His peace and strength to fill our trembling souls. If we are fighting fear or anxiety, let's just lift up our hand to Him and commit to hold on. Let's choose to walk by faith and not by sight (II Corinthians 5:7) until He takes us to glory, where we will be with Him for all eternity.

Just a Closer Walk with Thee

I am weak but Thou are strong;	Just a closer walk with Thee,
Jesus, keep me from all wrong;	Grant it, Jesus, is my plea,
I'll be satisfied as long	Daily, walking close to Thee,
As I walk, let me walk close to Thee.	Let it be, dear Lord, let it be.

Reading 24: Psalms 75-77   Incomprehensible

Who is so great a God as our God?
    You are the God who does wonders...   Psalm 77:13b, 14a

The sun rises every morning and sets every night, and we tend to think "Of course it does." But when was the last time we really tried to comprehend the incomprehensible wonders of creation?

Here are a few mind-boggling facts to ponder:

The sun is around 93 *million* miles away from earth.[xv] Can we even begin to fathom that distance? If we drove that distance at 65 miles per hour, non-stop, it would take a whopping 163 *years* to drive there! Even if we flew at 550 miles per hour, it would take nearly 20 years to arrive. Incomprehensible.

In completing its rotation once every 24 hours, our earth spins at a speed of about 1,000 miles per hour! How is it that this planet can be spinning at that speed, and yet we can experience perfectly still air and can walk around without feeling a thing? That wouldn't be the same experience if we were shot out of a cannon and hurtling through space at 1,000 miles per hour! Incomprehensible.

But that's not all. While our earth is rotating 1,000 miles per hour, it is also orbiting the sun at around 67,000 miles per hour. At the same time, the earth, the sun, and our entire solar system is circling around the center of the Milky Way galaxy at about 450,000 miles per hour! Plus, it is estimated that there are over 100 *billion* galaxies or more![xvi] Absolutely incomprehensible!

Our God spoke all of this into being with just the power of His voice (Genesis 1). When we feel overwhelmed by anything in this brief, temporary life on earth, let's shift our focus to the power and majesty of the God who has called us out of darkness into His marvelous light. As we intercede, we can entrust every detail of our lives to the One who not only calls all the stars by name (Psalm 147:4), but who numbers every hair on our head (Luke 12:7). Incomprehensible indeed.

Praise to the Lord, the Almighty

Praise to the Lord, the Almighty, the King of creation!
O my soul, praise Him for He is thy health and salvation!
All ye who hear, brothers and sisters draw near
Join me in glad adoration.

Then they remembered that God was their rock,
and the Most High God their Redeemer.   Psalm 78:35

When we first read this, we rejoice! They remembered! But, upon closer examination, we may become discouraged as we consider it in context.

This verse begins with *"Then* they remembered..." So what happened in the verse before? Verse 34 says "When He *slew* them, *then* they sought Him" (Psalm 78:34 – emphasis added). How sad it took calamity to get their attention. But are we any different?

God has miraculously rescued each one of us as believers from the slavery of sin. Yet, how often do we forget? How often do we not trust His higher ways? Why do we want to reject His direction and commandments, and go our own way, thinking we know better?

God knows that we tend to so easily forget who He is and what He has done. That is why He instructs a constant retelling of His works and His commands: "Teach them diligently to your children, and talk of them when you sit in your house, when you walk by the way, when you lie down, and when you rise up" (Deuteronomy 6:7) – in other words, *all* the time. What happens as we recount His wonders and His instructions? We also remind ourselves.

God also instituted "Memorial Stones", instructing that rocks be taken from the dry riverbed as reminders of His miraculous provision, and "the peoples of the earth may know the hand of the LORD, that it is mighty, that you may fear the LORD your God forever" (Joshua 4:24).

How can we create "memorial stones"? By sharing stories of God's faithfulness to us, journaling answered prayers, creating a "Faith Journal" for our children, or rereading Bible stories of God's miraculous provision.

Let's spend some time with the Lord today, reminding ourselves how He has miraculously delivered us. Let's ask Him to show us ways we can create "memorial stones" to remind not only ourselves, but generations to come, of His faithfulness.

Great Is Thy Faithfulness

Great is Thy faithfulness, O God my Father!
There is no shadow of turning with Thee;
Thou changest not, Thy compassions, they fail not;
As Thou hast been Thou forever wilt be.

Great is Thy faithfulness! Great is Thy faithfulness!
Morning by morning new mercies I see;
All I have needed Thy hand hath provided –
Great is Thy faithfulness, Lord, unto me!

...preserve those who are appointed to die;   Psalm 79:11c

In 2021, 3.5 million lives were lost worldwide to Covid-19.[xvii] In response to the threat of Covid, the world virtually shut down to preserve life. But was Covid-19 the leading cause of death in 2021?

Actually, no. Abortion was.[xviii] In 2021, there were 42.6 million abortions worldwide.[xix] There were over 10 times as many deaths from abortion than Covid. Where was the mobilization to preserve *these* precious lives?

People familiar with abortion will tell us an even more revealing truth: there are really two victims in abortion. Life is not only taken from a mother's womb, but life is also taken from her heart. Few people talk about a mother's heartbreak following an abortion, but guilt can haunt them for the rest of their lives.

Why aren't we doing more to stop this harm to so many women who feel they have no other choice except to take an innocent life? Is it because we don't really want to be bothered? We say "Oh, isn't that sad," but think "It's not my problem." Why is that? Is it because, deep down, we truly don't care about anyone else's life? Or have we been subtly influenced by the ways of the world?

As we pray today, Let's ask Him to show us His heart on this sensitive issue. Let's allow Him to burden our hearts for *both* mother and child involved in these challenging circumstances. Let's ask Him to show us how to use our time and resources to "preserve those who are appointed to die."

Let's remember that we all have been tricked by Satan's deceptions at various times in our lives. We all have sinned and fallen short (Romans 3:23). Together we plead, "Oh, do not remember former iniquities against us! Let Your tender mercies come speedily to meet us" (Psalm 79:8). Then, as Jesus did for the woman caught in adultery, may we not condemn, but give grace and lovingly say "Go, and sin no more" (John 8:11 NKJV).

Rescue the Perishing

Rescue the perishing, care for the dying;   Rescue the perishing,
Snatch them in pity from sin and the grave;   Care for the dying,
Weep o'er the erring ones, lift up the fallen,   Jesus is merciful,
Tell them of Jesus, the Mighty to save.   Jesus will save.

Reading 27: Psalms 82-85   Revival

Will You not revive us again, that Your people may rejoice in You?

Psalm 85:6

What a wonderful prayer for revival!

First, it reveals the proper motive in praying for revival – that we would rejoice in Him. Oftentimes, we tend to focus on ourselves instead of Him. We want things to go back to the way they were because our lives were more predictable and more comfortable.

But that ease of life may have been exactly what got us into trouble in the first place. We may have readily acknowledged the existence of God; we may have even felt we were truly worshipping and honoring Him. But the truth is, we didn't feel like we really needed Him.

However, with the growing upheaval in our own individual lives as well as the lives of many around our planet, we are becoming increasingly aware of our desperate need for Him. And that is exactly what He wants to accomplish, not only in our lives, but in the lives of people around the world.

Secondly, it acknowledges that revival comes from God alone, reminding us that only prayer can bring the change we desire. He alone is able to draw wayward hearts back to Him. This truth can help us as we pray over the spiritual condition of our country and the waywardness of those we love.

As we pray for revival, let's also include the Psalm writer's additional request: "But let them not turn back to folly" (Psalm 85:8d). What a waste of our fervent prayers if, in the end, people simply return to their selfish, foolish and ungodly ways. Peter talks of this pattern, warning that "the latter end is worse for them than the beginning. For it would have been better for them not to have known the way of righteousness, than having known it, to turn from the holy commandment delivered to them" (II Peter 2:20-21). May these truths encourage us and give us direction as we fervently intercede today.

Revive Us Again

We praise Thee, O God, for the Son of Thy love,
For Jesus who died and is now gone above.
Hallelujah, Thine the glory! Hallelujah, amen!
Hallelujah, Thine the glory! Revive us again.

Reading 28: Psalms 86-88   An Undivided Heart

Give me an undivided heart, that I may fear Your name.

Psalm 86:11

If we need to ask God for an *undivided* heart, we can assume that it does not come to us naturally. We likely more easily identify with a *divided* heart, torn between two opposing affections such as good and evil, or obedience and disobedience.

This is the same struggle Paul addressed when he said "For the good that I *will* to do, I do not do; but the evil I will *not* to do, that I practice. O wretched man that I am! Who will deliver me...? Only Jesus Christ, our Lord!" (Romans 7:19, 24-25)

The truth is, we are born with a heart that is totally inclined to evil, that is "desperately wicked" (Jeremiah 17:9). But when God calls us "out of darkness into His marvelous light" (I Peter 2:9), He creates a desire in our hearts to want to please Him. But we still struggle with wanting to please our flesh. Our heart is torn, divided.

In contrast, an undivided heart is one that is united in its direction of affection. It turns its focus first to God's kingdom and His righteousness, and leaves the rest to Him (Matthew 6:33). Whenever "the worries of this life and the deceitfulness of riches" try to choke out our faith (Matthew 13:22), an undivided heart will fight to bring its focus back to His kingdom and His righteousness. A united heart also allows us to wholeheartedly seek His face in intercession on behalf of others, and will produce an abundance of fruit for the kingdom.

As we intercede today, Let's ask Him for an undivided heart so that we will remain focused on the awesomeness and faithfulness of our Almighty God. No matter what uncertainty, fear and upheaval is going on in the temporary circumstances of our lives, our undivided heart can bring us back to a focus on this eternal truth – we have an All-Mighty, All-Knowing, All-Sovereign God who is on our side (Romans 8:31).

I Surrender All

All to Jesus I surrender,	I surrender all,
All to Him I freely give;	I surrender all;
I will ever love and trust Him,	All to Thee, my blessed Savior,
In His presence daily live.	I surrender all.

*I will sing of the mercies of the Lord forever...*Psalm 89:1a

Mercy is not a commonly used word today, so what exactly does it mean? It means not getting the punishment we justly deserve. What do we deserve? Death. Why? Because we all have sinned, and the penalty for sin is death (Romans 3:23; 6:23).

Today's Psalm says "righteousness and justice are the very foundation of His throne" (Psalm 89:14). Therefore, it is absolutely impossible for God to turn a blind eye to sin. We would like Him to, but that is not at all biblical. The righteousness and justice of God require the penalty of death for sin be paid, and paid *in full.*

We can only begin to appreciate the magnitude of God's mercy as we try to comprehend the immensity of His righteousness. God is total purity. He is completely righteous and always just. Therefore, He takes unrighteousness (sin) very seriously. How seriously?

God is so serious about sin that He sent *Himself,* in the form of the Son, to live a perfect, sinless life among us, and suffer the agony of the worst death imaginable, in order to satisfy His *own* wrath and judgment against sin. What a magnificent plan by which both His righteous justice could be met and His infinite mercy shown.

Have we ever really taken the time to ponder this truth? Because of His great love for us, God *Himself* took on our sins and paid our penalty of death in order to redeem us and restore us to a right relationship to Him. How incomprehensible!

As we read Psalm 89 and engage in battle today, let's remember that there is no hope for anyone without Jesus. No one can earn their own salvation or work their way to heaven. We all have sinned, but Jesus paid it all. "The *gift* of God is eternal life through Christ Jesus our Lord" (Romans 6:23b). If we confess to Him that we are sinners and receive His gift of eternal life, we also will sing of the mercies of the Lord *forever!*

I Will Sing of the Mercies

I will sing of the mercies of the Lord forever, I will sing, I will sing;
I will sing of the mercies of the Lord forever, I will sing of the mercies of the Lord.
With my mouth, will I make known Thy faithfulness, Thy faithfulness,
With my mouth will I make known Thy faithfulness to all generations.
I will sing of the mercies of the Lord forever, I will sing of the mercies of the Lord.

Whoever dwells in the shelter of the Most High
will rest in the shadow of the Almighty.   Psalm 91:1

Imagine for a moment a rushing waterfall. Take in the sights and sounds of the crashing, powerful water, coming wave upon wave. But then, on closer observation, you notice a little bird settled on her nest behind the waterfall. In spite of the turmoil and noise around her, she has found a place of security and protection, a place of peace.

This image is similar to what the Psalmist describes in Psalm 91. No matter the circumstances swirling around us, we can choose to dwell "in the shelter of the Most High." And the result? We will experience "rest in the shadow of the Almighty." Rest in the shadow of the Almighty. Now that is truly a place of peace. What greater place of security and protection could there be than resting "in the shadow of the Almighty!"

We tend to think of peace as the absence of turmoil. But the peace that God gives is most profoundly experienced in the presence of turmoil. Jesus told us to expect trials and troubles in this world. That is the nature of our brief life on this earth. But what else did He say? He said that we can find our peace in Him, because He has overcome the world (John 16:33).

As we stand firm in our faith and engage the enemy in battle today, let us remind ourselves that "from everlasting to everlasting", He is God (Psalm 90:2b). Regardless of any circumstance we face, we can choose to dwell in the shelter of the Most High, and rest in the shadow of the Almighty.

And how can we stay in that place of peace? By continually giving thanks and singing praises to Him; "to proclaim Your love in the morning, and Your faithfulness at night" (Psalm 92:2). This turns our focus from the temporary turmoil of this world to our peace and rest promised in the shelter of the Most High.

Like a River Glorious (v. 2 & 3)

Hidden in the hollow of His blessed hand,
Never foe can follow, never traitor stand;
Not a surge of worry, not a shade of care,
Not a blast of hurry touch the spirit there.

Every joy or trial falleth from above,
Traced upon our dial by the Sun of Love;
We may trust Him fully all for us to do -
They who trust Him wholly find Him wholly true.

Stayed upon Jehovah, hearts are fully blessed –
Finding, as He promised, perfect peace and rest.

When anxiety was great within me,
Your consolation brought joy to my soul.   Psalm 94:19

When circumstances start to fill us with fear, what consolations can calm our anxious minds and bring joy to our souls? The very first absolute bedrock of truth is "Be still and know that I am God" (Psalm 46:10). When anxiety begins to disturb our peace, this verse can quickly quiet our souls.

What else casts out fear? Perfect love (I John 4:18). Who has perfect love for us? Our Lord and Savior, Jesus Christ. And "neither death nor life, neither angels nor demons, neither the present nor the future, nor any powers, neither height nor depth, nor anything else in all creation, will be able to separate us from the love of God that is in Christ Jesus our Lord" (Romans 8:38-39). *Nothing* can separate us from His love. Period.

Then let's remember that He alone knows the beginning from the end and every moment in between. He declared "I am the Alpha and the Omega...who is, and who was, and who is to come, the *Almighty*" (Revelation 1:8 – emphasis added). What a statement of power! *Nothing* is too difficult for Him (Jeremiah 32:17), and *nothing* takes Him by surprise. And He is coming again!

In the meantime, He has promised to work all things out for our good because we love Him, and are called for His purposes (Romans 8:28). He called us; He *chose* us (John 15:16). This truth is such a comfort. Because He chose us, He will preserve us until everything He has planned for us has been fulfilled! (Psalm 138:7-8 ESV) Period.

As we read our Psalms to Him and intercede today, let's praise Him for all the truths He has given us in His Word. And when anxiety tries to sneak in to destroy our peace and steal our joy, let's send it sprawling as we defeat it with our sword of truth, His Word. Rejoicing because He has overcome the world (John 16:33), let's cast all our cares on Him because He cares for us (I Peter 5:7).

All the Way My Savior Leads Me

All the way my Savior leads me; what have I to ask beside?
Can I doubt His tender mercy, who thru life has been my guide?
Heav'nly peace, divinest comfort, here by faith in Him to dwell!
For I know whate'er befall me, Jesus doeth all things well;
For I know whate'er befall me, Jesus doeth all things well.

Reading 32: Psalms 97-101   Faith

Worship the LORD with gladness;
*   come before Him with joyful songs.*   Psalm 100:2

Today's Psalms recount the power of God: He reigns; He preserves; He delivers. He is victorious; He answers; He executes revenge. He is our Creator; we are His sheep; He is our Shepherd. In response, we are told to rejoice, sing praises, give thanks; shout joyfully, exalt and praise His holy name.

But sometimes, we just don't feel like praising Him. We look around and it seems that He is not present. We turn to Him but don't see answers, not even on the distant horizon. We feel as if our prayers go into a great void with no one there who cares.

What we need is a major dose of truth.

So let's ponder this for a minute: Is there such a thing as air? Of course! But have we ever actually seen even a speck of air? No. But we see what air does. We smile as leaves shimmer in the breeze; we watch clouds float lazily across the sky; we are mesmerized as snowflakes dance in the frosty air.

It's no different with God. Though we haven't yet seen Him physically, the effects of Him are all around us. We can look back at how our sins brought us to our knees, and how He raised us up to new life in Him. We know He removed our selfish heart of stone and gave us a heart of love for Him and compassion for others (Ezekiel 36:26). And it's not like we haven't had miraculous answers to our prayers. We just forget to remind ourselves about them.

So how do we move beyond doubt and despair? We take action. As we intercede today, we remind ourselves that we walk by faith and not by sight (II Corinthians 5:7). We determine, regardless of our feelings, to "be thankful to Him, and bless His name." Why? Because, this is truth: "The LORD *is* good and His love endures *forever*; His faithfulness continues through *all* generations" (Psalm 100:4-5).

My Faith Has Found a Resting Place

My faith has found a resting place -   I need no other argument,
Not in device nor creed;   I need no other plea;
I trust the Everliving One -   It is enough that Jesus died,
His wounds for me shall plead.   And that He died for me.

88

Reading 33: Psalms 102, 103   Dust

As a father has compassion on his children, so the LORD has compassion on those who fear Him; for He knows how we are formed, He remembers that we are dust.   Psalm 103:13-14

Some of us may be offended by being considered "dust". But these verses can actually be comforting. Why? Because we don't have to pretend, or perform, or prove anything. He has chosen to love us just because we are His, and nothing can separate us from His love (Romans 8:38-39).

Sometimes, in trying to be a better follower, we can become self-focused. We begin evaluating our actions, measuring our performance through our own eyes, and then can struggle with pride in our accomplishments. It makes us realize, no matter how hard we try, we will never meet God's standard. In and of ourselves, our "goodness" will never "earn" us salvation.

Does that mean we should not even try to please Him? No, but it changes our motivation. We can strive to please Him like a child desires to please a parent. Of course, sometimes we think we know better about what is best, silly children that we are. But after getting bruised from bumping into reality, we can run back to Him.

What a wonderful picture of the relationship we have with Him, our all-knowing, all-wise, all-loving Father. As His child, if we recognize that we are no longer walking in obedience, we can come running back, tell Him we're sorry, and He takes us back immediately. Why? Because He knows we are dust. And He has chosen to redeem and love us just the same.

As we come to Him in prayer today, let's come as His little child. Let's thank Him for accepting us, not because we are perfect, but simply because He has chosen us to be His. Then, out of gratitude for His love and mercy, we can aim to love and please Him with all our heart, with all our soul, with all our mind, and with all our strength (Mark 12:30).

Savior, Like a Shepherd Lead Us

Savior, like a shepherd lead us,	Blessed Jesus, blessed Jesus,
Much we need Thy tender care;	Thou hast bought us, Thine we are;
In Thy pleasant pastures feed us,	Blessed Jesus, blessed Jesus,
For our use Thy folds prepare.	Thou hast bought us, Thine we are.

Reading 34: Psalm 104, 108   Sing

I will sing to the Lord all my life;
I will sing praise to my God as long as I live.   Psalm 104:33

There is something so very powerful about songs of praise. They allow our spirits to rise above our circumstances. They can bypass our emotions as our focus moves from ourselves to the truth of their words. They can lift a heavy heart out of a pit in almost miraculous and instantaneous ways.

The great reformer, Martin Luther, declared "Next to the Word of God, music deserves the highest praise. The gift of language combined with the gift of song was given to man that he should proclaim the Word of God through music."[xx]

Song can reaffirm truth and minister to our souls unlike any other method. We can try looking at nature, and conclude that there has to be a God. We can read Scripture and agree that it is truth for our lives. But we sometimes can still struggle with translating that "head" knowledge into "heart" knowledge, having it impact the deepest part of our lives. Often times, our hurt, confused, or troubled emotions can block that journey. But singing can transform our emotions and minister truth directly, bringing comfort and healing to our deepest need.

Pastor Charles Swindoll has said of the hymns: "For long centuries, its soothing strains have calmed anxious hearts, incited courage in the fainthearted, comforted the grieving, healed the wounded, rescued the perishing, and drawn wanderers home."[xxi]

No matter what may be troubling our souls today, let's choose to sing praise to Him in the midst of these troubles. As we read the Psalms to Him, let's join in praising Him for His mighty deeds. As we stay our minds on Him, He promises us perfect peace (Isaiah 26:3). Then let's take His peace that "transcends understanding" (Philippians 4:7) into our intercession, confident that He is on His throne awaiting our requests so that His Hosts can be released to accomplish His will, in His time and in His way.

I Will Sing the Wondrous Story

I will sing the wondrous story,	Yes, I'll sing the wondrous story,
Of the Christ who died for me -	Of the Christ who died for me;
How He left His home in glory,	Sing it with the saints in glory,
For the cross of Calvary.	Gathered by the crystal sea.

Reading 35: Psalm 105

Remember

Look to the LORD and His strength;
Remember the wonders He has done.   Psalm 105:4a, 5a

When facing difficult, painful or anxious circumstances, we tend to look to ourselves and our own strength. We can feel helpless and hopeless as our eyes focus only on our circumstances. Our minds become filled with fear, doubt and despair. That's why the Psalmist instructs us to "Look to the LORD and His strength."

But how can we move our eyes from ourselves to the Lord and His strength? By filling our minds with all the *wonders* He has done.

He is the God of all creation, who simply spoke the entire universe into being. He is the God who, with mighty signs and wonders, led His people out of Egypt and into the promised land. He is the God who chose to come down to earth to live a perfect life among us and die an unspeakably agonizing, substitutionary death so that we could be credited with His righteousness and live forever with Him.

When we turn to Him in repentance and accept His free gift of salvation, He is the God who chooses to live in and through us. He is the God who reaches down into each of our lives, redeemed us, and continues to draw us into intimate relationship with Himself. He is the God who promises to never leave us nor forsake us, who promises that nothing and no one can separate us from His love. This is the God we serve!

As we engage in battle today, let's remember that He alone is the God of wonder, power and might! Nothing is a surprise to Him and nothing is impossible for Him (Matthew 19:26). Let's release to Him any fear about where He is taking us or what our future holds. Let's also remember that, as we cry out to Him in fervent prayer, His answers may be the stories of miracles that will be told for generations to come, because He alone is the God of wonders.

I Sing the Mighty Power of God

I sing the mighty pow'r of God,
That made the mountains rise,
That spread the flowing seas abroad,
And built the lofty skies.

I sing the wisdom that ordained
The sun to rule the day;
The moon shines full at His command,
And all the stars obey.

Reading 36: Psalm 106 Mission Possible

Yet He saved them for His name's sake,
to make His mighty power known. Psalm 106:8

Have we ever stopped to think about what God's purpose was in saving us? We tend to think it's all about us: "He saved me from the penalty of my sin"; "He saved me so I could go to heaven;" "He saved me so I could have a better life here on earth." But according to Psalm 106:8, His purpose was "to make His mighty power known."

How can we make His mighty power known? First, we can share our testimony about how He saved us. I Peter 2:9 tells us to "declare the praises of Him who called you out of darkness into His wonderful light." But then it instructs "Live such good lives among the pagans…that they may see your good works and glorify God" (I Peter 2:12). We are to live such exemplary lives that nonbelievers will give glory to God for our good works and godly life. Now, that's a tall order!

Remember Mission Impossible? As Christians, our mission - which we have chosen to accept - is not about us. It's solely about bringing *Him* glory. But how can we remember to do that in our daily lives?

Let's try this: Think "Pleasing Him" as we consider our myriad of choices each day. We can even add a question mark: "Pleasing Him?" as we evaluate each decision about our language, our dress, our attitude, our business practices, our relationships, our priorities for time or resources. This phrase helps brings our focus back to Him and our mission in life.

Let's ask the Lord to help us remember why He saved us. As we apply "Pleasing Him" to each decision, prepare to be amazed at how quickly this phrase can help our "walk" match our "talk". But let's also be prepared to experience what peace and joy it brings to our days as we constantly and consistently remind ourselves to stay on mission: "to make His mighty power known."

Take My Life and Let It Be

Take my life and let it be	Take my love – my Lord, I pour
Consecrated, Lord, to Thee;	At Thy feet its treasure store;
Take my moments and my days,	Take myself and I will be
Let them flow in ceaseless praise,	Ever, only, all for Thee,
Let them flow in ceaseless praise.	Ever, only, all for Thee.

Reading 37: Psalms 107, 110   Redeemed

Whoever is wise, let him heed these things
and consider the great love of the LORD.   Psalm 107:43

We often say "People need to come to the end of themselves." We might even think this is a new concept. But this idea goes all the way back to the time of Psalms. Psalm 107:4-28 details multiple examples of people coming to the end of themselves:

Some "wandered in desert wastelands," hungry and thirsty. *Then,* they cried out to the Lord and He delivered them. Some "sat in darkness and the deepest gloom" because they rebelled against God's Word. *Then,* they cried out to the Lord and He saved them.

Some "became fools through their rebellious ways and suffered affliction because of their iniquities; ...they drew near the gates of death." *Then,* they cried out to the Lord and He healed them and "rescued them from the grave." Others were caught up in storms and "were at their wits' end." *Then,* they cried out to the Lord and He rescued them.

Doesn't this sound like people today? The Lord gathered these – His redeemed – "from east and west, from north and south" (Psalm 107:3). It reminds us of "a great multitude that no one could count, from every nation, tribe, people and language, standing before the Throne and before the Lamb. And they cried out in a loud voice: "Salvation belongs to our God, who sits on the Throne, and to the Lamb" (Revelation 7:9-10).

We are told that this countless multitude are those "who have come out of the great tribulation." "Never again will they hunger; never again will they thirst." and "God will wipe away every tear from their eyes" (Revelation 7: 14, 16, 17).

What an encouragement as we go into intercession today! There are countless people from every nation, tribe and tongue that have yet to come to the end of themselves, cry out to God, and be redeemed. They are why we have answered this call to battle. May we fight on with renewed intensity!

Redeemed

Redeemed, how I love to proclaim it!	Redeemed, redeemed,
Redeemed by the blood of the Lamb;	Redeemed by the blood of the Lamb;
Redeemed through His infinite mercy,	Redeemed, redeemed,
His child, and forever I am.	His child, and forever I am.

Reading 38: Psalms 109, 111, 112 Words of Life

Glorious and majestic are His deeds;
He has caused His wonders to be remembered; Psalm 111:3a, 4a

Mention "David and Goliath", and most everyone knows the story. From Creation through Revelation, we find recounted many "glorious and majestic" deeds of our God Almighty. Through the Bible, God has caused His wonders to be remembered for thousands of generations!

Some people say the Bible is so old, it must have been corrupted with time. But the Dead Sea Scrolls, discovered in 1947, demonstrate that, because of reverence for God's commands, our current Old Testament is incredibly accurate. The first century Jewish historian Josephus explained, "For, although such long ages have now passed, no one has ventured either to add, or to remove, or to alter a syllable; and it is an instinct with every Jew from the day of his birth to regard them as the decrees of God."[xxii]

The accuracy of our New Testament is upheld by the volume of ancient manuscripts that, with remarkable consistency, recount the Apostles' eye-witness accounts and teachings. James MacDonald documents, "There are now more than 5,600 ancient manuscripts of the Greek New Testament. Add to that nearly 10,000 Latin manuscripts and 9,300 other early versions, and we have nearly 25,000 early manuscripts of the Bible. No other ancient document even comes close. The next most commonly copied document is Homer's *Iliad*, with 643 manuscripts, all of them partial. Thus, the Bible manuscripts outnumber those for Homer by nearly forty to one."[xxiii]

Although the Bible is the most authenticated, copied and most-read book of all time, people will still question its authenticity and authority. But we have every reason to trust it as the divinely inspired Word of God, remarkably preserved so that His wonders are remembered. As we read our Psalms to Him today, may we treasure His gift that has been faithfully passed down through the ages. May His glorious and majestic deeds bolster our courage as we intercede today. What a mighty God we serve!

Wonderful Words of Life

Sing them over again to me, wonderful words of Life;
Let me more of their beauty see, wonderful words of Life.
Words of life and beauty, teach me faith and duty;
Beautiful words, wonderful words, wonderful words of Life;
Beautiful words, wonderful words, wonderful words of Life.

Reading 39: Psalms 113-115   Hallel (Part 1)

Who is like the LORD our God,
  the One who sits enthroned on high...   Psalm 113:5

Our Psalms for today and tomorrow are known as "The Hallel". "Hallel" simply means "Praise" and is similar to the English word, Hallelujah, "Praise Yah" or "Praise Yahweh".

In our first three Hallel Psalms today, the recurring theme is praising the name of the Lord. Specifically, we are led in praising Him for who He is, for what He has done, and for what He will do.

First, He is "exalted over all the nations, His glory above the heavens" (Psalm 113:4). There is no one like our God. Therefore, we are not foolish to worship Him, because He is God Almighty, the creator and ruler of the entire universe!

Secondly, He has done great things in our lives. Psalm 114 talks about bringing His people out of bondage in Egypt. Similarly, each one of us can look to our own lives and praise Him for how He has brought us out of our own bondage to sin and rebellion. Additionally, He gave us a heart that desires to please Him above all else. Indeed, He has done great things!

Thirdly, Psalm 115 talks about what He will do. "You who fear Him, trust in the LORD – He is their help and shield" (Psalm 115:11). This describes His rescuing us and defending us – both offense and defense. What more could we ask for! He is *everything* we need in every circumstance of life.

As we come before Him today, let's follow these Hallel psalms and simply praise Him. He is always and forever enthroned on high, and we praise Him for who He is. He has done great things in our lives and the lives of others, and we praise Him for what He has done. He has promised to be our help and our shield, so we praise Him for what He will do. "It is we who extol the LORD, both now and forevermore" (Psalm 115:18). It is all about Him.

Joyful, Joyful, We Adore Thee

Joyful, joyful, we adore Thee,
God of glory, Lord of love;
Hearts unfold like flowers before Thee,
Opening to the sun above.

Melt the clouds of sin and sadness,
Drive the dark of doubt away;
Giver of immortal gladness,
Fill us with the light of day.

Reading 40: Psalms 116-118   Hallel (Part 2)

Give thanks to the LORD, for He is good;
His love endures forever.   Psalm 118: 1

Today's reading is the second half of the six Psalms known as "The Hallel". The word "Hallel" is short for the Hebrew phrase "Hallelu Yah", which translates as "Praise the LORD".

The Hallel Psalms played a significant role in many of the Jewish holidays, but particularly in the Passover celebration. A portion of them would typically be sung prior to the Passover meal, and the remaining would be sung after the meal.

Most scholars believe that today's psalms were sung by Jesus and His disciples after the Last Supper, a Passover meal, before they walked to the Mount of Olives and the Garden of Gethsemane, where Jesus would be betrayed, arrested and ultimately crucified (Matthew 26:30).

As we read Psalms 116-118 to the Lord today, let us remember that Jesus sang these same Psalms as a hymn of praise. Unlike the disciples, He was fully aware of the pain and suffering He was about to endure. For us. So that by His stripes, we could be healed. With His crucifixion, the debt of our sin has been paid *in full* (Isaiah 53:5). And with His victory over death in His resurrection, we are raised to new life in Him (Romans 6:4).

As we approach the Throne of Grace today, may we move our eyes from our temporary troubles to the transcendent truth that "His love endures forever." Regardless of our immediate circumstances, we can know that "His love endures forever." We may not begin to grasp why He allows the trials we are facing, but we can know that "His love endures forever." With Job, we can say "Though He slay me, yet will I trust in Him" (Job 13:15 NKJV). And this we can know for certain: "You, O LORD, have delivered my soul from death" (Psalm 116:8), so we can join the countless multitudes in the heavenly chorus singing, "His love endures forever."

The Love of God

The love of God is greater far,   The guilty pair, bowed down with care,
Than tongue or pen can ever tell;   God gave His Son to win;
It goes beyond the highest star,   His erring child He reconciled
And reached to the lowest hell;   And pardoned from his sin.

O love of God, how rich and pure! How measureless and strong!
It shall forevermore endure – The saints' and angels' song.

Reading 41: Psalm 119:1-56   Owner's Manual

Open my eyes that I may see wonderful things in Your law.
Psalm 119:18

Psalm 119 was written to celebrate God's law. But when we first encounter the word "law", our initial reaction is usually not one of celebration. Why? Because we immediately think someone is trying to tell us what we *can't* do. That's why we need the Lord to open our eyes, so we can see His law as a wonderful thing, something to help us live our best life possible.

Let's think back to when we bought our first car. We pored over the owner's manual to learn how the car was designed and how to best utilize the newest and latest features. How arrogant it would be to disregard the owner's manual and think "Well, I don't need any instruction. I can figure it out myself."

It's the same way with us. God designed us and knows far better how we function best. That's why He inspired, and preserved, His owner's manual – the Bible - so we could live our most productive and fulfilled life.

As we think back to the times when we chose to do it our way, doing what felt right to us, we ended up down a destructive path. Why? Because His ways are higher than our ways. Because He is God and we are not. Because His mind is infinite and ours is not. So we need to study and commit to His ways, not ours. The question is not "Does His way make sense to me?" The question is only "Is this His way?"

As we read today's portion of Psalms to Him, may we embrace its truth with our whole heart. Then, let's commit to follow His guidance in obedience, walking by faith and not by sight, and turn that strengthened faith into fervent intercession. As we line up our lives with His instructions in His owner's manual, we will experience the blessings of doing things His way, because His Word alone gives us life (Psalm 119:50 NKJV).

Open My Eyes, That I May See

Open my eyes, that I may see
Glimpses of truth Thou hast for me;
Place in my hands the wonderful key
That shall unclasp and set me free.

Silently now I wait for Thee,
Ready, my God, Thy will to see;
Open my eyes – illumine me,
Spirit divine!

97

Reading 42: Psalm 119:57-112   Affliction

It was good for me to be afflicted
so that I might learn Your decrees.   Psalm 119:71

We all want our lives to be trouble-free. Why? We think we deserve it. After all, we are doing our best to follow Him and do His will, so why should we have to suffer the heartbreak of wayward spouses or children, the pain of persecution, or the sorrow of the loss of health or life?

The truth is that trials are not something we can prevent, even though, consciously or subconsciously, we often rehearse all the details in our minds and wonder what we could have done differently. We are missing the point.

In our focus verse today, affliction is praised for teaching us to look to His ways, depending on Him instead of ourselves. Hebrews 12:11 further elaborates: "No discipline seems pleasant at the time, but painful. Later on, however, it produces a harvest of righteousness and peace for those who have been trained by it."

Scott Hubbard of desiringgod.org writes: "I would like to think I could have made it safely to heaven on a smooth path, running straight and wide beneath bright skies. I would like to imagine I would remain faithful to God without the training rod of trouble. But in a world like ours, and with hearts like ours, some of God's best gifts come wrapped in the black box of trouble. They burden us, sometimes almost unbearably. But they also bend us toward the One whose steadfast love is better than life (Psalm 63:3)."[xxiv]

Whatever troubles we are facing, our sovereign God has allowed them for His divine purposes. Let's ask Him to help us be soft clay in His Potter's hands, as He forms us into useful vessels to carry and reflect His glory. May we see that these trials are causing us to "become mature and complete", so that we will be able to "count it all joy" (James 1:2 NKJV). In the end, He is our portion (Psalm 119:57). He is all we need.

It Is Well with My Soul

When peace, like a river, attendeth my way,   It is well
When sorrows like sea billows roll -   With my soul;
Whatever my lot, Thou hast taught me to say,   It is well, it is well,
It is well, it is well with my soul.   With my soul.

Reading 43: Psalm 119:113-176   Embrace the Reins

Direct my footsteps according to Your Word;
let no sin rule over me.   Psalm 119:30

Imagine a horse and buggy. The driver wants to get home with the least amount of time and energy. He wants to be efficient.

The horse has no idea what the goal is or how to get there. He just wants to go his own way and look for grass or a shady place to lay down.

Without the reins and direction of the driver, the horse may never get home to the safety of the stall, to food and water, and to the pleasure of pasture in the cool of the evening.

Both we and the horse often resist the idea of reins. We think that, without reins, we will be able to get to the same destination in the same amount of time, but by taking our own path and experiencing the pleasure of our own willfulness along the way.

If we are honest, our willful ways always get us into trouble. Have they ever truly led to peace and fulfillment? Or did they lead us into heartache and heartbreak, addictions and pain?

As we look around, our hearts break as we see the chaos and despair that result from throwing off His reins in willful rebellion. Sadly, while we as Christians know better, there are many who don't even know the way. They have never experienced the blessings of being under His authority and His direction.

As we spend our last day in Psalm 119, may our hearts be filled with gratitude to God for His law, our reins. And may we entreat Him to restore across our country an appreciation for His reins. He designed us. He alone can lead us in the way we should go. May our lives be examples to others of the benefit of embracing His reins. May we clearly demonstrate that He alone can be trusted, in the midst of the uncertainty and struggles of this life, to efficiently and effectively lead us home.

He Leadeth Me

He leadeth me! O blessed thought!
O words with heav'nly comfort fraught!
What e'er I do, where e'er I be,
Still 'tis God's hand that leadeth me.

He leadeth me, He leadeth me,
By His own hand He leadeth me;
His faithful foll'wer I would be,
For by His hand He leadeth me.

Reading 44: Psalms 120-126   Crosses

Those who sow in tears will reap with songs of joy.   Psalm 126:5

We probably all can recite the words of Jesus: "Whoever wants to be My disciple must deny themselves and take up their cross daily and follow Me" (Luke 9:23). We hear that and think, "Yep, we need to take up our cross and follow You, Lord." And He promises that His yoke is easy and His burden is light (Matthew 11:30).

Then why doesn't it feel light? Is it because we are carrying the burden of other people's crosses? What about that spouse who has stopped going to church? Or that son or daughter who has become a prodigal? Or the grandchildren who show no interest in spiritual things. Are we carrying their crosses, too?

Yes, we should care about their spiritual waywardness. Yes, we should take it as a burden to the Lord, but then leave it there. Easier said than done, right? Yes, but we can ask the Holy Spirit to show us when we are taking it back, trying to find a way to fix it, or worrying about their eternal destiny.

We need to continually remind ourselves that no amount of worry, argument, logic, pressure, manipulation, or emotional appeal is going to change them. Why? Because it is a matter of the heart. And only God can change a heart.

As we read our Psalms to the Lord today, let's praise Him for the promise that those who sow in tears will reap with songs of joy. And as we intercede on behalf of those we love who have wandered off in sin, let us remember that the most loving and effective thing we can do for them is to bring them to The Cross. In doing fervent battle on their behalf, we may end up sowing in tears. But then we can rejoice, because we have brought them to the One Who can transform their hearts. And in our waiting, let's remember Jesus' promise: "Come to me, all you who are weary and burdened, and I will give you rest" (Matthew 11:28).

Near to the Heart of God

There is a place of quiet rest,	O Jesus, blest Redeemer,
Near to the heart of God,	Sent from the heart of God,
A place where sin cannot molest,	Hold us who wait before Thee
Near to the heart of God.	Near to the heart of God.

Reading 45: Psalms 127-132   Not Fair

If You, O LORD, kept a record of sins, O Lord, who could stand?
But with You there is forgiveness...   Psalm 130:3-4a

Life is not fair. Some people have more, some have less. Some people are born into riches, others into poverty. Some people are smarter than others. Some gals are prettier; some guys are more athletic. Life just isn't fair. So why do we say life should be fair, when we know it never can be?

If we really stop to think about it, what we really mean is that we want things to be better in our lives and the lives of those we love. Honestly, when we complain that life isn't fair, we seldom mean that we have too much, that we have been more blessed than others. It's usually that we think we deserve more, we deserve better.

The cold, hard truth is this: We should be thankful that we don't get what we deserve. If we only got what we deserved, Jesus never would have suffered and died to pay the penalty for our sins. We would never have received forgiveness, or be given second chances to come back to Him time and time again.

What we deserve is to be left dead in our trespasses and sins. What we deserve is eternal damnation. What we deserve is to suffer the consequence of every rebellious thought, word and deed. If life were truly fair, we would all be equally condemned, equally miserable, equally lost, equally forever separated from God.

Let's be thankful that life isn't fair. As we come to Him today, let's rejoice that He chose to redeem us and restore us to relationship with Him, the Almighty Creator of heaven and earth. "For it is by grace you have been saved, through faith – and this is not from yourselves, it is the gift of God" (Ephesians 2:8). How truly unfair is that! Then let's fervently intercede as He continues to draw many others into that "unfairness", His kingdom of Truth and Light.

And Can It Be That I Should Gain?

And can it be that I should gain,	Amazing love! How can it be
An int'rest in the Savior's blood?	That Thou, my God, shouldst die for me?
Died He for me, who caused His pain?	Amazing love! How can it be
For me, who Him to death pursued?	That Thou, my God, shouldst die for me?

Reading 46: Psalms 133-135; 137, 138   Preserved

Though I walk in the midst of trouble, You preserve my life;
* the LORD will fulfill His purpose for me...* Psalm 138:7a-8a ESV

These verses from Psalm 138 can bring such comfort. No matter what circumstances we face in life, we can trust Him to preserve our life until His purposes have been fulfilled. Nothing and no one can interfere with His plans for us.

But sometimes we aren't exactly on board with His purposes for us. Why? Because if we had our way, we wouldn't choose to walk "in the midst of trouble".

That's when it helps to remember the truth: This life is no longer about us, our comfort or our pleasure. Now that we belong to Him, our life is all about fulfilling His purposes for us and bringing Him glory. Sometimes, "trouble" allows us to shine for Him. Other times, He uses "trouble" to prune and train us so we can mature and be more fruitful for Him.

Those of us who garden know that consistent fertilizing, weeding, and pruning are necessary for a fruitful harvest. Left untended, a garden can quickly fill with weeds that choke out everything else.

The same is true of our human heart. Left to our own devices, we have a natural bent to sinful ways, to "weeds". We should not be surprised when "sin sprouts" pop up in our lives. A daily check-in with our master Gardener is a great way to keep those sprouts from taking over. It certainly is less painful and less disturbing to our hearts and lives if plucked out as a little sprout than if we allow it to flourish and become a stronghold.

We will always be in need of our master Gardener, our Redeemer and our Lord. As we read these Psalms to Him today, let's rejoice that He preserves us until His purposes are fulfilled. And as we intercede for each other and our nation, let's welcome His tender tending, so we can bear more fruit for His kingdom.

God Leads Us Along

In shady, green pastures, so rich and so sweet,
God leads His dear children along;
Where the water's cool flow bathes the weary one's feet,
God leads His dear children along.

Some thru the water, some thru the flood,
Some thru the fire, but all through the blood;
Some thru great sorrow, but God gives a song,
In the night season and all the day long.

Reading 47: Psalms 136, 139   Trust

You are familiar with all my ways. Before a word is on my tongue
you know it completely, O LORD.   Psalm 139:3-4

Today's focus verses are some of the strongest statements in Scripture about the intimate knowledge God has of each of us. Can we even begin to imagine that, before we even speak a word, He already knows it *completely!* Even though it is beyond our ability to grasp, it isn't any less true.

This truth can help us face the unknown in our lives, particularly the uncertainty of our futures between now and the moment we are received by Jesus into heaven.

The Holocaust survivor, Corrie Ten Boom, had many moments of fear in the face of an uncertain future. In *The Hiding Place*, she shares the story of her father's response when, as a child, she tearfully told him of her fear of his death: "Father sat down on the edge of the narrow bed. 'Corrie,' he began gently, 'when you and I go to Amsterdam - when do I give you your ticket?' I sniffed a few times, considering this. 'Why, just before we get on the train.' 'Exactly. And our wise Father in heaven knows when we're going to need things, too. Don't run out ahead of Him, Corrie. When the time comes that some of us will have to die, you will look into your heart and find the strength you need - just in time.' "xxv

Corrie also shares this encouragement: "When a train goes through a tunnel and it gets dark, you don't throw away the ticket and jump off. You sit still and trust the engineer."xxvi

As we read Psalms 136 and 139 to the Lord today, let's remember that our Engineer is totally trustworthy. He already knows whether or not what we fear will ever happen. If it does, He will give us the strength to face it. Nothing is a surprise to Him. He alone knows every detail of every moment of our lives. He can be trusted.

I Must Tell Jesus

I must tell Jesus all of my trials,	I must tell Jesus! I must tell Jesus!
I cannot bear these burdens alone;	I cannot bear my burdens alone;
In my distress He kindly will help me,	I must tell Jesus! I must tell Jesus!
He ever loves and cares for His own.	Jesus can help me, Jesus alone!

Reading 48: Psalms 140-143   The Joy of Surrender

Show me the way I should go, for to You I entrust my life.

Psalm 143:8

Reading Psalms 140 through 143, it's impossible not feel David's anger and fear. He is being hunted down just because he stepped out in faith, slew a giant, and became an overnight sensation.

As He cries out to God, his words reflect his anxiety. But, after all his pleading for God to change his circumstances - as well as rain down destruction on his enemies - he says "Show me the way I should go, for to You I entrust my life." He has finally come to that joyous point of surrender.

Joy in surrender? Isn't surrender just a sign of weakness and admission of failure? How could there possibly be joy in surrender?

Joy actually can most often *only* be found on the other side of surrender. Let's consider that thought a moment.

Proverbs 3:5 says we should trust Him whole-heartedly instead of our own understanding, our own way of doing things. Here's an example: Jesus tells us to love our enemies and pray for those who persecute us (Matthew 5:44). That makes no sense to us. "They don't deserve it!" They don't. But when we surrender to His way, we find hatred, bitterness and anger can be washed away with a flood of peace and joy.

His way gives us a different perspective. As we release our enemies to Him, we remember this life is just temporary. He may have a greater purpose in this situation than we could ever see with our own eyes. It allows us to find rest, joy and peace in Him, our sovereign Redeemer and Lord.

As we read through David's complaints and pleas today, let us follow his example and, in the end, lift up our soul to Him in prayer, surrendering all to His way and His will. With Jesus, may we pray "Your will be done" (Matthew 26:42), and then rest in the joy of surrender to Him and His ways.

Leaning on the Everlasting Arms

What a fellowship, what a joy divine,	Leaning, leaning,
Leaning on the everlasting arms;	Safe and secure from all alarms;
What a blessedness, what a peace is mine,	Leaning, leaning,
Leaning on the everlasting arms.	Leaning on the everlasting arms.

The Lord is gracious and compassionate,
        slow to anger and rich in love.   Psalm 145:8

Because our God is gracious, compassionate, slow to anger and rich in love, He is patient. As we look back, we see how He has been so patient with us as we struggled to come to, and stay in, dependence on Him. Yet, we often fight impatience when we don't see immediate answers to our prayers.

If we believe we are trusting Him, then why do we fight impatience? Is it because we don't *really* trust Him to accomplish it in *His* time, in *His* way, and in *His* plan? Are we thinking "God, I have such a good plan. It's in keeping with Your will. Why aren't You doing my plan as I have asked it to be done?"

Though we don't realize it, what we may be saying is "My will be done." Take our prayers for the return of our prodigals, for example. It's a good will. We want what He wants. And it is for the eternal benefit of those we love. However, we are frustrated that we don't see the answer – now already.

We say we trust Him to accomplish it in His time. But in the meantime, we worry. Maybe part of what we want is for God to answer our prayer so we feel that we don't need to worry anymore. As if our worrying can accomplish anything. No, Jesus tells us not to worry (Matthew 6:25-34).

And maybe we haven't truly let go so that He is free to do His work.

As we read our Psalms to Him and intercede once more, let's make sure we have handed them over, *totally* handed them over, to His perfect plan. Let's look ahead to the future when they will be returned to the fold, and then spend time thanking Him for the way in which He is answering our prayers. He *is* working out all the details in their lives for His glory. Because, in the end, it is all about His glory.

Be Still, My Soul

Be still, my soul – the Lord is on thy side!	Be still my soul – Thy God doth undertake
Bear patiently the cross of grief or pain;	To guide the future as He has the past;
Leave to thy God to order and provide -	Thy hope, thy confidence let nothing shake -
In ev'ry change He faithful will remain,	All now mysterious shall be bright at last,
Be still my soul – thy best, thy heav'nly Friend	Be still my soul – the waves and winds still know
Thru thorny ways leads to a joyful end.	His voice who ruled them while He dwelt below.

Reading 50: Psalms 147-150   Facing the Future

He counts the number of the stars; He calls them all by name.
                                    Psalm 147:4 NKJV

We can tell ourselves that we are not afraid of the future. We can recite verses telling us not to fear. We can remind ourselves that, regardless of what the future holds, our eternal destiny is secure. And yet, fear of the future can loom large when we see God allow a difficulty, sadness, or loss in someone else's life. What if God calls us to suffer similar challenges, trials, or tests? And fear can begin.

We tell ourselves that we just want to be ready in case the worst should happen. But what we are really trying to do is be God. We want to see into our future. Ultimately, what we are doing is entertaining the great deceiver, whose fearful whisperings are intended not to warn and prepare, but instead to kill, steal, and destroy.

Our enemy wants to kill our dependence and our trust in God. He wants to steal our peace and our joy. He wants to destroy our witness by moving our focus from the God of Peace to the fear of potential circumstances. How many times have we anticipated grief or braced for the worst, only to have it not happen? How much joy and peace have we forfeited? How productive for him, but how counter-productive for us.

As we lift today's Psalms of praise to our Almighty God, let's remind ourselves that He counts the stars; He alone calls them all by name. Let's rejoice that He already knows all our future, every single moment He has planned for each one of us. There is no place for fear.

In intercession, let's stand firm in our faith, with our armor in place. Let's raise our shield of faith, quench that fiery dart of fear and send it back to the pit of hell where it came from. Then let's boldly march forward and reclaim surrendered territory, remembering it is all about Him, His purposes, His kingdom and His glory.

Blessed Assurance

Blessed assurance, Jesus is mine!
O what a foretaste of glory divine!
Heir of salvation, purchase of God,
Born of His Spirit, washed in His blood.

This is my story, this is my song,
Praising my Savior all the day long;
This is my story, this is my song,
Praising my Savior all the day long.

GOING FORWARD

*For I am not ashamed of the Gospel of Christ, for it is the power
of God to salvation for everyone who believes.*

Romans 1:16 NKJV

What's Next?

We have been faithful to answer His call to "stand in the gap" on behalf
of our nation.

We have completed the 31 Days of Preparation prior to battle. We
prayed and fasted on New Year's Day as the Lord led. We stood firm,
engaged the enemy, and brought praises, prayers and petitions to the
Throne of Grace for 50 days. Now what?

Hopefully, we have been drawn closer to our Lord though this process,
are walking with a renewed spirit and refreshed heart now more full of faith,
and encouraged in the truth that prayer changes things.

Let's continue to keep our swords sharpened by committing to stay in
the Word, choosing to follow its wisdom and direction as our moral
compass instead of leaning on our own understanding. Let's continue using
our powerful weapon of prayer to bring about the changes He desires, both
in our hearts as well as in the hearts and lives of those we love.

Let us truly become His people again, a people who reflect and resemble our gracious and forgiving Heavenly Father. Let's offer the Lord our bodies as cleansed and useful vessels for His blessing, using our resources to be the hands and feet of Jesus in our needy world. Let's be a passionate people who are not just talking about, but actually living out the "good news", as a testimony that speaks not only to our next-door neighbor but, together, reaches around the globe, impacting generations to come.

As we move forward, let's ask the Lord to show us precisely how He wants to continue to bring change not only to our individual lives, but to the lives of our families, our businesses, our churches, our schools, our communities and to all levels of leadership in our nation.

As His eyes continue to search "to and fro throughout the whole earth" (II Chronicles 16:9 KJV) looking to support those whose hearts are fully devoted to Him, may He see us, faithfully continuing to "stand in the gap". May we continue to ask Him for renewal of our hearts, restoration of His place on the throne of our lives, and revival in our land.

For God so loved the world that He gave His one and only Son, that whoever believes in Him shall not perish but have eternal life. For God did not send His Son into the world to condemn the world, but to save the world through Him. Whoever believes in Him is not condemned, but whoever does not believe stands condemned already because they have not believed in the name of God's one and only Son. This is the verdict: Light has come into the world, but people loved darkness instead of light because their deeds were evil. Everyone who does evil hates the light, and will not come into the light for fear that their deeds will be exposed. But whoever lives by the truth comes into the light.   John 3:16-21

May we continue to bring our lives to the transforming light of His truth.

If we will…then He will.

Bibliography

How Did We Get Here?? – page 4

[i] George Washington's 1789 Thanksgiving Proclamation - www.mountvernon.org/education/primary-sources-2/article/thanksgiving-proclamation-of-1789/

The Power of Prayer – pages 9-11

[ii] www.historyonthenet.com/when-patton-enlisted-the-entire-third-army-to-pray-for-fair-weather

[iii] Msgr. James H. O'Neill, "The True Story of the Patton Prayer", 1950, (From the Review of the News, 6 October 1971)

[iv] Ibid.

[v] Ibid.

[vi] Ibid.

[vii] Public domain – published and distributed by the United States Army, 1944

December 14 – page 28

[viii] Christ-Centered Mall, www.christcenteredmall.com/teachings/armor-of-god-2.htm

December 15 – page 29

[ix] Dave Johnson, "What is the Breastplate of Righteousness?", www.lifehopeandtruth.com/change/christian-conversion/armor-of-god/breastplate-of-righteousness/

[x] www.gotquestions.org/breastplate-of-righteousness.html

Preparation Day 31 – page 45

[xi] Priscilla Shirer, "A Life in Alignment", Passion Conference 2018, January 5, 2018

[xii] Walt Disney Pictures, *The Lion King*, 1994

New Year's Day – A Time of Prayer and Fasting – page 47

[xiii] Wayne Grudem, *Systematic Theology: An Introduction to Biblical Doctrine* (Grand Rapids: Zondervan, 1994, 2000), p. 391

Reading 20 – page 76

[xiv] https://buffalonews.com/news/ogrady-recounts-survival-rescue-f-16-fighter-pilot-sobs-as-tape-of-first-radio-contact/article_4934e5f0-0034-5c04-a9d9-455a

Reading 24 – page 80

[xv]https://spacemath.gsfc.nasa.gov › weekly

[xvi] Louie Giglio, *How Great Is Our God: 100 Indescribable Devotions about God and Science*, (Nashville: Tommy Nelson, 2019) pp. 36-37

Reading 26 – page 82

[xvii] decisionmagazine.com/abortion-the-leading-cause-of-death-in-2021/, quoting statistics from Worldometer.com and the World Health Organization.

[xviii] Ibid.

[xix] Ibid.

Reading 34 – page 90

[xx] Martin Luther, as quoted by Charles R. Swindoll, *THE HYMNAL for Worship & Celebration*, (Waco: Word Music, 1986) Foreword

[xxi] Ibid.

Reading 38 – page 94

[xxii] Josephus, *Contra Apionem* I.37–44, as cited in Dunkelgrün, T. The *Testimonium Flavianum Canonicum*: Josephus as a Witness to the Biblical Canon, 1566–1823. *Int class trad* 23, 252–268 (2016). https://doi.org/10.1007/s12138-016-0408-4

[xxiii] James MacDonald, *God Wrote a Book*, (Wheaton: Crossway, 2002, 2004), p. 18

[xxiv] Scott Hubbard, https://www.desiringgod.org/articles/better-to-have-a-burden, 09/12/2022

Reading 47 – page 103

[xxv] Corrie Ten Boom, *The Hiding Place*, (New York: Crossings Classics, 1971, 1984), p. 27

[xxvi] Corrie Ten Boom Quotes. BrainyQuote.com, BrainyMedia Inc, 2022. https://www.brainyquote.com/quotes/corrie_ten_boom_393675